CREDIT

REPAIR

SECRETS

A Proven System That Allowed 12.771 People to Repair Bad Credit in 27 Days, Including

LUCAS ANDERSON

Credit Secrets

7 Strategies to Raise your Credit Score Fast, Repair your Negative Profile and Get Out of Debt to Finally Change Your Financial Life

[LUCAS ANDERSON]

Legal & Disclaimer

The information contained in this book and its contents is not designed to replace or take the place of any form of medical or professional advice; and is not meant to replace the need for independent medical, financial, legal or other professional advice or services, as may be required. The content and information in this book has been provided for educational and entertainment purposes only.

The content and information contained in this book has been compiled from sources deemed reliable, and it is accurate to the best of the Author's knowledge, information and belief. However, the Author cannot guarantee its accuracy and validity and cannot be held liable for any errors and/or omissions. Further, changes are periodically made to this book as and when needed. Where appropriate and/or necessary, you must consult a professional (including but not limited to your doctor, attorney, financial advisor or such other professional advisor) before using any of the suggested remedies, techniques, or information in this book.

Upon using the contents and information contained in this book, you agree to hold harmless the Author from and against any damages, costs, and expenses, including any legal fees potentially resulting from the application of any of the information provided by this book. This disclaimer applies to any loss, damages or injury caused by the use and application, whether directly or indirectly, of any advice or information presented, whether for breach of contract, tort, negligence, personal injury, criminal intent, or under any other cause of action.

You agree to accept all risks of using the information presented inside this book.

You agree that by continuing to read this book, where appropriate and/or necessary, you shall consult a professional (including but not limited to your doctor, attorney, or financial advisor or such other advisor as needed) before using any of the suggested remedies, techniques, or information in this book.

Table of Contents

Introduction

A good credit score plays a vital role in helping you maintain your financial condition. Most Americans do not understand what a credit score is all about. It's now evident that a lot of Americans are yet to know the importance of maintaining or improving their credit score even if they are not hoping to apply for the loan in the future. The important thing here is that regardless of whether you take a loan or mortgage now or in the future, it is necessary to have a good credit report. Not having this can deny you access to make big purchases such as cars and houses because oftentimes, your loan's interest rate is determined by your credit score. A really low or bad score does not only affect your rates but can lead you into serious trouble if not immediately addressed.

It is better to have a good credit score at the beginning and maintain it than to have a bad score and try fixing it because to fix your credit score; it is a function of who you give to help you fix and also the information you open yourself to. Because depending on if you spend thousands of dollars to have it fixed or go-ahead to fix it by yourself, you might hurt your credit report even more, hence causing more harm than good.

Chapter 1: The Importance of Good Credit Score

Obtaining the valuable credit score goes a long way to make a choice on if the funds should be loaned or not. This also helps these entities that want to extend credits to know the precise amount of money to give the person as well as with what interest rate.

Experian, Equifax, and TransUnion are the three most common credit reporting agencies. Each of these companies offers a free credit report individually, making it a total of three reports per year. From this, you can tell that it is necessary that one reads and understands the contents that are on the report. Information such as errors in the amount of money to be paid back, payment histories and errors in late payment content can be seen. It also helps to confirm that there is no identity theft in the report.

Companies offering credit will be cautious in taking a closer look at numbers on the credit score of an individual. Lenders believe that a score of 700 or above is a very excellent one. One should value keeping their scores high at all times because there seem to be several advantages of obtaining a high credit score. Credit extensions having low-interest rate offers would definitely be secured by the high scoring report owners. Moreover, for those with high credit scores, credit approval processes are normally done super-fast (in little or no time).

Before applying for a big loan, it is important to note that the one who wants to credit is expected to screen their report at least up to six to twelve months approximately. Checking the score helps you see for yourself that the details are listed correctly and fish out errors that may not seem to tally. In a case where there are errors, the period earlier mentioned allows the one seeking credit to properly address the errors that may have occurred. In a case where errors on the report still surface at the time of applying for a large loan, it is still critical that the lender is made aware of these mistakes depending on the situation.

Just as this book teaches, it is possible to improve your credit score. One of the ways this can be done is ensuring you pay all owed money on a regular basis hence reducing your outstanding account balances. Since deadlines of payments are noted on every report, it is always best to pay in good time. For the borrower's sake, it would be advisable not to take on new debt.

To round this up, here are a few things I'll mention that point you to receiving a good credit score:

Speaking with creditors and credit advisors will be a major advantage for you as there are cases where one might be faced with a really terrible financial crisis where payments cannot be made within that time. The creditors would most likely be ready to assist to the best of their ability, especially when it comes to lowering and spreading out payments.

Do not allow your credit card balances go to the roofs. Making them as low as possible is vital. I do not advise you to let them go high.

One thing that makes me laugh about some people is that they think they can improve their credit score by simply just closing their old accounts, so they hide late payments displayed on those accounts. It doesn't work that way. The late payment history will still show on the credit report, even if that account is closed.

Lenders always check to see the credit history with active borrowing of previous years or more.

Achieving a good credit score range might not be easy at first, but it will go a long way to boost your personal financial life. All this must be done with a sense of keen insight as well as careful thinking.

Chapter 2: How Credit Score is Calculated

The credit score is calculated using several pieces of your credit report. If you want to have a high credit score or have good credit, you must know how it is calculated and what factors (banks and credit agencies) to take into account to approve or deny a loan or credit card. Your credit score is calculated based on these categories, namely:

· The amounts that you owe

· The history of Payment

· What types of open accounts you have

· The age of the accounts

· The number of credit applications

Let's examine these factors and see how we can raise your credit score one by one.

1. The amounts that you owe

It is no coincidence that the amounts that you owe is the next thing to discuss. This is because, after the history of payment, it is known to be the next most influencing factor of your credit score.

It is already a general rule that you are required to use only 30% of the credit the bank approves to you and nothing more than that. It will be highly unwise if you go ahead to use all the credit that the bank approves, say $300 on a $1000 credit card. That means you should never make use of the maximum account that has been allowed on your card. Credit bureaus perceive this as an omen when you start to depend on the money and they tend to withdraw as it signifies a negative mark for your credit report and also your credit score.

I would advise you to use below 30% of your credit, or what's best if you could go-ahead to use only 10% of your credit line and nothing more than that. By doing this, you will have better credit scores and your chances of increasing and even sustaining a good credit score will be limitless.

The amount of money that you owe is also a key factor to consider when calculating your score.

2.   The history of payment

Consider making payments on or even earlier than the agreed time as it is absolutely important and has a major impact on your score. If you are one that makes late payments, then your credit score will dramatically reduce.

The fundamental thing a lender would want to find out is whether or not you paid your bills or even your credit loans in a good time. This category out of the others majorly influences your credit score and makes up to 35% of your score, which is why it is very important to take note of it.

Now that you know that delayed payments can affect your credit score and also hinder you from building a good credit history, you must do well to ensure you pay all debts on time without any qualms.

The types of accounts normally considered for payment history are namely:

- Installment Loans
- Credit Cards (such as Visa, Master Card and so on)
- Loans to the consumer
- Retail accounts and;
- Mortgage Loans

Remember, the path of making and building a good credit score is a path that will require you to make payments on time.

3. What types of open accounts you have

Another factor that can favor your credit score is having various types of loans (mortgages, cars, and student loans) and credit cards.

Your credit score is majorly concerned with the different types of credit that you use, some of which exist are credit cards, mortgage loans, installment loans and accounts with finance companies too.

Do take note that it is not so important that you use each one of them and I'll advise that you only open accounts that you really are going to use.

The credit mix has no major effect on your credit score, but it is of great importance that your credit report does not contain excess information on which your score is based.

As it were, there is really no perfect version of a credit mix as it varies with time from individual to individual. Opening car loans, student loans and credit cards you won't be needing won't be advisable for you. Although, it would be an added advantage to have this factor that shows that you know how to handle your credit responsibly.

4. The age of the accounts

Consistency is key in the credit score world. As long as you keep maintaining a good credit score history, your credit score will always remain high. The general rule explains it as the longer you have credit cards, the more your credit score increases. That's why I'll advise you to start your credit as soon as you can. This is a factor that constitutes about 15% of your credit score, measuring the length at which you have your credit accounts and how well you have been able to manage them within that period.

Here are what your FICO credit score records:

·   It takes into account the age of both the new and old accounts and even an average age of all of your accounts.

·   It also takes into account your credit lines (if you have), how long you have been with them and how your payment history has been.

· And finally, it measures the exact age of your loans/credit cards. Because of this, many professionals advise that older accounts should neither be closed nor canceled as it is likely to affect your credit score. There's a high possibility of you having a high credit score by having a long time with your credit.

5. The number of credit applications

Lastly, the number of applications to your credit slightly affects your credit score. Every time you apply for a loan or possibly a credit card (even if not yet approved), your credit score slightly decreases.

Opening various credit accounts within a very short time can be very risky for financial institutions, most especially when it's a case of one who does not have a lengthy credit history. This explains why many people see that their credit score has decreased either when they open a credit card or approved for a particular loan. However, the decline is temporary.

Also, bear in mind that credit checks vary. Interestingly, checking your credit will have your credit score reduced if and only if it is a hard inquiry. There are hard inquiry and soft inquiry of which I will explain below.

The hard inquiry is made when a loan is applied with a lender. That may include a student loan, car, mortgage loan. These inquiries affect your credit score.

While the soft inquiry is made when you request a copy of your credit report, apply for a job or maybe use it for a credit monitoring service. These types of inquiries in no way affect your credit score.

How exactly is it calculated?

As important as it is to calculate your credit score, it is also very important to know that these factors have no fixed percentage as they may vary due to the financial information obtained from your credit report.

This goes to say that without adequate knowledge of the basic factors above, there is a tendency for an individual to be careless in the decisions he makes at obtaining a high credit score. It is hence very important that these factors are known.

Though these factors are applied when calculating a credit report, the level of importance varies from person to person.

It is not possible to record the impact of each of the factors on the credit score without acknowledging the report as a whole.

How to check your credit score

Some services enable you to check your credit score at very little or no cost. However, you must take caution and use services that you know are reliable, so you don't fall into the hands of scammers on the Internet. Some of these reliable services, especially the ones listed below, have no cost.

Some of these services are:

Experian: - This US credit agency is used by several lenders to evaluate your credit and requires you to pay just $1 to view your credit.

TransUnion: - This credit bureau also allows you to see your score quickly and easily. It is also used lenders as well as banks to estimate your credit.

Quizzle: - This is a credit score simulator that offers a Vantage Score that is based on TransUnion data.

Mint.com: - This is another simulator that utilizes data from the Equifax credit agency.

Credit cards that allow you to see your credit score

It is also very possible to obtain your credit score for FREE by having some particular credit cards at your disposal. Asides the bonus reward you get, these cards improve the quality of your credit score and notify you immediately there is any form of suspicious activity. Here are two that I can guarantee are simply the best.

Discover IT credit card

Discover IT credit card is known to be one of the best credit cards of recent. This card uses Experian data to display your credit score monthly.

Monthly, your credit tracker is updated, notifying you of sudden changes in your credit report. Also, it is accepted internationally and is relatively easy to obtain.

CreditWise from Capital One

The Capital One credit cards feature the CreditWise credit simulator which uses TransUnion data to give you a weekly evaluation of your credit score.

It allows you to predict and calculate a cause-and-effect situation if you paid all debts or made payments on time for either 6 or 12 months and so on.

It is available to Capital One bank customers using any of their credit cards.

Chapter 3: The Right Way to Check your Credit Report

The business uses the credit and pays the bill promptly. As the business has established a positive business credit profile, and as the business continues using the credit and paying the bills on time, it will qualify for more credit.

The first step in business credit building is for the business owner to order a credit report for the business. It is very important for the business owner to know what really is being reported for that business in regard both to positive and derogatory information. The business owner will also want to actively monitor the business credit building and score building as it is taking place.

Business Credit Reports

Many business owners find, when they receive their Business Information Report from D&B, that they have a low PAYDEX score. They scratch their heads and wonder why their score is low even when they are paying the bills on time.

A business owner cannot find out which companies are reporting negative information to your file without having a credit report. However, a business owner can obtain a list of all the companies that are reporting to the business credit file. Upon request, the business owner will get an alphabetical list of all the companies reporting to the business credit bureau as well as the number of times they reported.

On page 2 of the report will be an overview of the companies that have reported and the dollar-weighted payments. The Paydex score will also be on the report. Each of the companies listed will be sorted by supplier industry. If there are less than 20 companies on the list, the D&B

representative might choose to simply read the list over the phone or e-mail the information to the business owner.

Other information on this report includes the total dollar amount of all trades reported, the largest amount that anyone trade has reported, and the percentage of payments that have been made to the top ten (10) industries.

The Experian Smart Business credit report will tell the business owner how many trade lines are reporting and show if a business credit score has been assigned if the business has an active Experian Business Profile, and if the business has had any recent credit inquiries.

Once a business sets up its credit report and pays some bills on time, it should have a high PAYDEX score. It is then vital that the business maintain its report.

The business owner should check the business report periodically. They may want to consider purchasing the Monitoring Service that D&B offers. This service allows a business to receive alerts when new positive or negative information appears on the report. There are several areas that a business owner will be notified of if they change including:

- ☐ Credit Rating
- ☐ Suits, liens or business judgments
- ☐ PAYDEX score changes
- ☐ Changes to financial statements
- ☐ Other significant business news

It is extremely important that the business credit file remain accurate. The Fair Credit Reporting Act does not apply to businesses as it does with consumer reports. If there is something wrong on the business credit report, or if a step is skipped in setting it up, there is no legal recourse to have that information removed. If the file was set up incorrectly, there's a good chance the business credit file could be put in the "High Risk" category, making it nearly impossible to remove inaccuracies.

This is your Credit Scorecard as of 05/20/2016. Come back after 30 days to refresh it.

740	28	2 years	21	1%	0
FICO SCORE	Total Accounts	Length of Credit	Inquiries	Revolving Utilization	Missed Payments

Your FICO® Score based on
Experian data

740

FICO® Scores range
from 300 - 850

How lenders
see your score

Very Good

FICO® Scores in the range of 740 - 799
are considered very good

Your FICO® Score compared to the
U.S. average by age

See what's affecting your FICO® Score

↑ What's helping

↓ What's hurting

Chapter 4: How to Repair Your Negative Profile

Where to Start Repairing Your Credit

If you realize that your score is low, there are certain drastic measures you need to take in order to address the situation.

-Stop using credit cards. If your circumstances demand that you must use a credit card at some point, use the credit cards with the lowest interest rate. Cheap is the catch phrase for you now because you are trying to resolve a credit score crisis. It has a lot to do with your spending habits.

-Deposit as much as you can to the cards that charge the highest interest. Just meet the minimum for the other cards in the meantime. This is one of debt recovery strategies. It is more like an inverted snowball approach.

-Don't open new credit accounts as you are trying to repair your damaged credit score rating. Don't jump from one problem to the next. New credit accounts will simply lead you down the same road of destruction as has happened in the current situation.

-Avoid opening new credit accounts in a short span of time. This often happens when you are looking for funding for college. Although some agencies have a waiver for such enquires if they are done within a span of a month, others still consider such applications and factor them in your credit report. You are therefore advised to spend a much shorter time shopping for funding for your college fees. The exceptions notwithstanding, such acts are generalized considered an indication of poor financial management.

Let's take a look at the strategies you can use to repair your credit.

Identify theft claim

Over 16 million Americans are victims of identity theft. This is definitely a large population so anyone could be a victim. Identity theft is a crime which involves the police so ensure you are ready to go this route. If you are sure that your score has been ruined because of identity theft, you can use this method. Abusing this method could land you into trouble with the law. Here is how to dispute using the method:

Step 1: Report the matter to the police then get a copy of your report from the local sheriff (you will need this report later)

Step2: File the dispute with FTC using this link **here**.

Step 3: Go on to dispute with various credit bureaus.

Step4: Set up an identity theft alert (be sure to know what this means in terms of your access to credit).

Pay the original creditor

You don't want multiple collection agencies reporting new items every month since this hurts your score. Simply send a check with full payment of the outstanding amount to the original creditor then send proof of the payment to the collection agencies that have reported that debt. After that, you then request that they should delete all the derogatory items from your credit report. You can blend this with the pay to delete strategy mentioned above.

Pay to delete

In this strategy, you agree to pay a creditor only if they agree to delete such items from the credit report. I mentioned about zero balances; don't fall for the trap of creditors who say they will mark it as zero. Zero is not good for you because it shows you have been having problems in the past (this sticks in your credit report for 7 or more years)! In simple terms, your report shouldn't be showing that you have had a bad credit history with derogatory items. If the creditor is interested in their money more than tainting your credit, they will agree to this. If the information passes to collection agencies after 2 years, you can also use this strategy to make them stop reporting your settled debt; in any case, they buy the debts for a tiny fraction so anything they get will probably be good enough! This is the best time (when the debt is with the collection agencies) to use the pay to delete strategy because you have more bargaining power. If the collection agency doesn't accept your offer, its only option is through a judgment.

Note#1: Use pay to delete when you start noticing new derogative items in your report since these could easily hurt your credit. You might even start seeing multiple collection companies reporting the same debt. In such times, you have an advantage since you negotiate everything on your terms; if one does not accept your offer, another will definitely take it.

Note#2: Have everything put in writing if they agree on your terms. If they cannot put it in writing, don't pay. After paying, you should give it about 45 days to reflect in your credit report. Don't take anything less than deletion; don't accept updating balance. If they cannot delete, don't pay. The process is pretty fast so they shouldn't give you excuses that they cannot delete; mention the Universal Data Form to make them know that you know that it is possible.

Note#3: Choose your battles well i.e. Don't use this strategy on creditors who have a lot to lose because they might sue you to compel you to pay. Aim for creditors who have already been barred by statute of limitation (2 years have passed), which means they cannot sue you in court to compel you to pay.

Settle your debt

Total debt owed accounts for up to 30% of the credit score so don't overlook this. This includes personal loans, car loan, and credit utilization. You should also calculate the credit utilization ratio (the balance you carry in your revolving fund compared to your credit). As your credit utilization increases, your credit score goes down; aim to keep your credit card balances no more than 30% of your credit card limit. You should even aim for zero balances since this means higher credit score. Combine this strategy with pay to delete strategy.

To pay your debts, you can use the snowballing or avalanching strategies. Snowballing involves paying off debts with the lowest balance first then closing them as you move up to the bigger debts. Avalanching involves paying debts starting from those with the highest interest rates as you move down.

Lookout for errors in the report

I mentioned that 93% of the credit reports have been proven to have errors. Look out for any of these then file a dispute. Such things like last date of activity, write off date, wrong account name or number and others could be enough to taint your credit. Don't overlook any of that. If the report really has an error, don't be discouraged by the credit bureau's stalling tactics; mention the Notice (Summons) and complaint to make them know that you are really aware of what the law requires of them. The bureaus wouldn't want to have their systems investigated and proven to be weak/flawed so this strategy can actually compel them to correct errors thus boosting your credit.

Mix/spread your credit

This usually affects your credit score by up to 10%. Having more types of credit signifies that you can handle your finances properly making you credit worthy especially if you have a good payment history.

Request for proof of the original debt

If you are sure that the credit card has been written off due to late payment, there are times when the carriers might not have the original billing statements within 30days as stipulated by the law. With this, you can get the item removed from your report such that it appears as if the entry was not even there. You can also request for the original contract that you actually signed when applying for a credit card. You shouldn't just ask for verification because by doing so, you ask the collection agency to verify that they received your request for collection on an account that bears your name. You should be clear on what you want them to do; in this case, they should provide proof of debt including giving you statements for the last few months and the original contract, which you signed.

Handy tips to improve your score

*Avoid Bad Signals

One of the subtle indications that your report may pick and affect you negatively includes using your credit card to a pawnshop. Although it is not an objective assessment of your financial situation, the readership will develop qualms about you. Such actions speak volumes about your financial organization ability.

*Do Not Delete Your Past Good Debt Records

Your credit history speaks volumes about your consistency. This is the information the lender looks for to decide whether you are a good or bad risk.

*Use fewer cards

The small nuisance balances on your cards adversely affect your score. Many people do not realize that it is more expensive to use more credit cards. It is even harder to manage them. Consequently, the chance of defaulting or making a late payment is significantly increased when you use several cards.

*Minimize the lowest interest rate loan hunt period

When you apply for many loans within a short period, the credit report often reflects several loans instead of the final one you might have settled on a month later.

*Get a settlement letter when you settle any debt then send the letter to the different bureaus to have any derogatory items removed.

Settle your bills promptly

Payment history accounts for 35% of your credit score making it one of the biggest determinants of the score. This is pretty straight forward; when you pay your bills on time, your score will improve. You could even set up automatic payments just to ensure that you won't miss payments since the amounts are deducted from your account. The biggest contributors to this include collections, bankruptcies, and different late payments. You should not that the recent delinquencies have greater effect than the old ones; 70% of the score is determined by whatever has happened within the past 2 years.

Watch out for Fair Debt Collection Practices Act (FDCPA) Violations

The law is on your side when it comes to the manner in which the debt collection agencies can collect debts from you. If they violate these, you can actually compel them to delete your derogatory entries since the penalties they will pay far exceed the amount that might be outstanding (some fines could go as high as $10,000). Actually, every violation has a penalty of $1000 payable to you! Here are some of the things to watch out for.

- If the creditor calls you before 8.00 am in the morning
- If they call after 9.00 pm
- If they call you at your place of work persistently
- If they call third parties. Creditors are only allowed to call your spouse apart from you for purposes of tracing you.
- If they inform someone else and inform them that they are trying to recover debt from you.
- If they call you after you have officially notified them not to call you.
- If they contact you after you have officially informed them that you are being represented by an attorney.

You can effectively defend yourself by reporting to the FDCPA if you are subjected to the following:

*If they try to collect invalid debt. This happens more frequently than most people know. It happens due to various reasons; some are deliberate while others are accidental. Some collection agencies try to take advantage and attempt to do a double collection

*If a collection agency agent lies or uses deceptive language.

NB: Since the use of the term deceptive is quite vague, you can take advantage and get yourself off the hook.

*If a debt collector leaves unclean messages on your answering machine. If they leave such a message, they must state that they are trying to collect debt. They must also leave their name and the name of the agency they are acting for.

*If they sue or threaten to sue after 4 years lapse after you attended to a debt. Note that the duration may differ in CA and a few other states.

*If they threaten and refer to being connected to a government agency courts or any law enforcement agent.

*When they threaten to sue you when they have no intention of doing so.

*If they threaten to garnish your income without explaining the due process. A creditor is supposed to file a suit and obtain judgment before they can garnish the income of debtors.

*If they sue you in another place other than where you live now and where you agreed

All you have to do to start the process is to tell them that you have been recording all their calls.

Chapter 5: How to Convert Bad Credit into Good Credit

Debunking eight common credit score myths

Loans have become a great tool that helps people solve their financial issues in no time. Although, beyond the several advantages and responsibilities, there are certain myths that we must be aware of and break. If you have plans to acquire a loan but are not sure if it's your best option, this book will show you how to see and handle the situation exactly as you should.

While some of us like credit score as it has favored us in our ability to handle it well, others see it as one that does more harm than good, which is not the case. The issue with people who do not enjoy the credit score is because they were misinformed on some things and it leads them to fall into traps they could have avoided if they had the right information all along. That's why in this section of this book, we will be discussing the eight common myths to break on credit score. These myths are:

1. When you close your many credit accounts, your credit score will improve

This may seem logically sound but is completely false. The way credit scores are calculated in parts is known as credit/ debt ratio. The agencies who calculate your score evaluate the amount of debt that you have and the amount of credit that is available for you to draw.

So let's assume you have ten credit cards and the credit availability all sums up to $100,000 and you have used only $15,000 of that available credit, your credit utilization rate becomes 15%. This is known as positive since you have 85% of your unused credit.

Let's take a case of you closing seven accounts because you're not using them. You will still have $15,000 in debt, but in this case, your sum total credit now available drops to $30,000. This means that your credit utilization rate has skyrocketed by 50%, hence your credit score dropping.

Do not close credit cards like this. It is better to put the cards away safely. And if there's a chance you can increase your credit limit, go for it. As long as you are not maximizing it, it will help your credit score.

2.   Once you have a bad credit score, it is impossible to get loans or credits

This myth has been derived from advertisements that require a good credit score to get funding. Interestingly, almost everyone can get funding no matter what their credit score may be, whether it is increased in the 800s or lower in the 400s.

What a credit score represents to financial institutions is a level of risk as this determines, to a large extent, the terms of any loan or credit received. Let's say, for example, someone who has a credit score of 800; the individual will be considered low risk for the financial institution. They already know that this person pays in good time, has available credit in high quantity and has longevity with his accounts. This will hence result in a low-interest rate and more credit available.

However, someone with a credit score of 450 will be considered high-risk. The reason is that the loans and credits will be available but will have oppressive interest rates for very little credits.

3.   Credit scores tend to change only a few times a year

Credit scores are usually in constant change. The information with which you calculate your score is derived from the financial institutions you maintain business relationships with. If you miss making a payment, it will reflect almost immediately. If you go ahead to close multiple accounts, the information will have an impact on your score much earlier than 3 or 6 months.

Looking at your credit score now, you can be able to see the latest updates that have been made. The time actually varies as sometimes it can be a matter of hours, than days or even weeks. Knowing this, you should ensure to check your credit score on a regular basis. So in case something bad happens, you can address it early enough.

4.   One thing that affects your score is the amount of money you make.

This is so not true. Your credit score does not list the employers' income but rather the credit accounts. So regardless of what you earn a year, whether you're a CEO who earns 3 million a year or an entry-level worker who earns $30,000 a year, your income does not determine your credit score. Interestingly, a wealthy CEO, even with so much money, might have a bad credit score because of bankruptcy or successions of late payments in the previous years.

The only way that your income can affect your credit score is if you live a Champagne lifestyle and having only a beer budget. That can be financially unhealthy for you. If it happens that you run out of your cards, by making minimum payments and losing them completely, your score gradually becomes a great success and peaks the top, as it should.

5.   Bringing a balance to your credit card also helps your score

No, not at all. To be quite frank, it doesn't hurt that either. But you would be wrong to think that keeping money on your card helps your score because it really doesn't. Ideally, I advise you to pay the balances on your cards fully every month in order to avoid paying interest on purchases. If you're just paying the minimum, then you're not doing yourself any good and wasting your money. Most of this minimum payment can be paid to the credit card company as only a small fraction pays the balance.

Do not bring a balance whenever possible. And if your balance exceeds 30% of your card, you should consider transferring from half to another card. When one-third of the credit is used on a card, then that can actually damage the credit score. In an ideal case, the balance ought to be less than 30% of the credit available; the lower it is, the better for you. This will be a good place to request a credit line increase, so as your line is increased by a few thousand dollars, your balance is affected and falls below 30%, hence increasing your credit score.

6. You can have an excellent credit report if you have no credit

The lack of credit is a good thing in some countries but not in the US. If you have never had a credit card or a car loan, you must be financially responsible. But as for the United States, your credit history determines your credit score. Good credit history equals a good credit score and vice versa.

All in all, credit scores are built. Financial institutions who lend loans and credits want to know that you will borrow money and payback on time coupled with an interest. Once they see that, then you are safe from any risk.

7. You can't recover from a bad credit score. It stays with you for life.

If you currently have a poor credit score, it is not the end of the world. If you are paying exorbitant interest rates now, you won't be doing so forever. Although repairing and rebuilding take time and patience.

Stick with the basics and be consistent with it. Open new credit lines and pay your credit card bills in time. Try to never miss a payment. Make your balances low at all times. Keep a very steady but low credit usage ratio. Do not apply to many cards or accounts in a year.

Once you can do these, even amidst all financial difficulties, your credit score will change for better.

CATEGORY	SCORE
Excellent (30% of People)	750 - 850
Good (13% of People)	700 - 749
Fair (18% of People)	650 - 699
Poor (34% of People)	550 - 649
BAD (16% of People)	350 - 549

Chapter 6: 7 Quickest and Easiest Strategies to Raise Your Score

Pay off what you owe

While this is going to be easier said than done in most situations, according to Experian, the ideal amount of credit utilization that you want is 30 percent or less. While there are other ways to increase your credit utilization rating, paying off what you owe on time each month will also go towards showing you can pay your bills on time, essentially pulling double duty when it comes to improving your credit score. It will also make it easier to follow through on the following tips.

Pay Bills The Day You Get Them

This might take some discipline but it's a great system to stay on track - pay your bills on the same day they arrive in the mail. If you have online banking, this will be quite easy: the bill arrives, you go to your computer or smart phone and log into your bank account, and you pay your bill. Done. One less thing on your mind and zero risk of being late with the payment.

Very often we are lulled into a false realty by bill due dates that are weeks away. You look at your account and think: I have a thousand bucks in there. Meanwhile you have three bills laying around for half of that amount. Your discretionary spending (wants, not needs) is quite different when you think you have X amount in your account rather than X minus bills. By paying your bills right away, you get them out of the way and won't forget to pay them. You are also going to spend less money because your account will be a more honest reflection of your financial picture.

It is incredible how easy it is to get into trouble financially when everything is payable in a month. We lose touch with where we really stand in terms of money. If you cannot afford to pay every bill as it

43

comes in, maybe take out a small loan to bring you to square one, and then chip away at the loan.

Get A Cash Secured Loan

Similar to the secured credit card, you can build and repair credit by taking out a cash secured loan. In this case, offer the bank to borrow x amount and use that amount as collateral on the loan. The funds will be locked down in a savings account and you will gain access to the borrowed funds once the loan is paid in full.

The advantage to the bank is that they have zero risk (they repay the loan with the savings if the deal goes south), they make a profit on the deal since the rate they pay on savings deposit is lower than the rate you pay on the loan, and the loan officer is happy about getting another sale. A good idea is to borrow an amount like $5,000 to $10,000 and repay it over the next 3 to 5 years with regular scheduled payments. As long as there are no late payments, this will count as a positive on your credit history. Do not repay the loan immediately, as you want the loan to run for a long time for maximum effect.

If the loan is repaid within a few months, it might not even have a chance of making a good impact on your credit score. As a bonus, once the loan is paid off, you will have access to the savings. This is often done by some creative lenders to help young people build credit and can be a forced savings plan for a future home purchase down payment.

Negotiate To Repay Written Off Items

Sometimes our mistakes are in the past and we are still paying for them in the present. Unpaid collections and written off loans and credit card balances not only look horrible on your credit history, they also lower your credit score immensely.

A write-off is basically when the lender decides that they have no chance of recovering the amount owed to them by you. They write-off the amount on their books and inform the credit bureaus. If you are able to do so, you should seriously consider paying any written off debts that you may have. You can often do so at favorable terms.

Call up the company that wrote off the debt and inform them that you would like to make amends by paying back some or all of the debt you owed them and that was written off. This will basically be free money for them as they have already made provisions for the loss. It makes the manager look good. Your condition should be that once the written off debt has been repaid by you, they will have to report to the credit bureaus and inform them of the change. Get this in writing and forward a copy of the letter to the credit bureaus. This will erase the negative entry on your credit history and make your credit score shoot upwards. If you are brave, you can also try to negotiate the amount it will take to remove the write off. Ask them to reverse any fees that might have been added over the course of the debt being delinquent. Sometimes they will also remove accrued interest from the debt and aim to recover only the initial amount owed to them less any payments made. You can also just bluff and say you only have x amount and are willing to pay that to them in return for the credit history adjustment. Sometimes, they will think that 40% recovered is better than 0% and go for it.

The point of all of this is that these things are not permanent and can be fixed if you are willing to make the effort.

When Rate Shopping, Do It Quickly

Every time there is an inquiry on your credit history, your score drops by about 10 points. If you are buying a new car or applying for a mortgage, you are likely to approach a few different lenders in order to get the best rate. Often their pricing is dependent on your credit score and they will need to view your credit history first before providing a quote.

When you are applying at only one bank, an inquiry is fine and won't affect your credit score much. It becomes messy though, when you have five or six different bankers taking a look over an extended period of time (one every weekend for instance). The credit bureaus understand that you might have to go through this process in order to get the best rate possible, they will not penalize you for multiple inquiries within a short period of time.

There is no specific time period in which to rate shop, but generally you don't want to be looking around for more than a week. Two weeks at the most if you want to take a risk.

Keeping all credit inquiries to within a short time period is a little easier done for mortgages since a house purchase is usually a very planned out process, and you can therefore stack a few mortgage appointments in one week. It is much harder when buying a car and applying for car loans to keep within a short time period. You might get pre-approved at your local bank, but then get roped into financing through the dealership when you finally find the right car a few weeks later. The local bank will pull a credit history and the dealership will send the loan application out to multiple lender, who will all likely look at the credit history again.

In order to avoid taking multiple hits to your credit score, try to wrap up your rate and loan shopping in a short period of time. There are also many banks out there that do not price your rate based on your credit score - these banks will be able to quote you a rate without pulling your credit history first. Once you officially apply for the loan, they will review the credit history for underwriting.

Avoid Over-Extending Yourself

People who live within their means usually have great credit. People who want to buy everything, and borrow every penny possible, usually have lousy credit. If you borrow too much, you will eventually run into problems making the payments. You can have a lot of debt and decent credit at the same time, but someday something might happen and cause the whole house of cards to fall down.

Often it takes a long time until problems become really obvious. Many people who have overextended themselves will keep things afloat for a while, usually by borrowing more and more. First they will forgo saving for retirement, then maintaining the house, then suddenly there is only enough to make the bare minimum payments on the credit cards and soon new debt is taken out to pay for old debt.

Banks will bail you out as often as they can because your banker is only a human and does not want to push you off the cliff. They will bail you out by giving more credit, and then some more until the day comes when there is no more room left. When that moment comes, the wall goes up and you are alone. Soon payments start coming in late and your credit score takes a nose dive. Once your credit history takes a hit, the chance of getting bailed out is going get even smaller.

For excessive debt to cause a lower credit score, you don't even need to be behind on payments. The amount you have borrowed and the level of usage of revolving credit, such as credit cards and lines of credit, can cause a drop in your score. At some point the credit bureau computer catches on that the big credit card balances aren't really going down month over month. It might just decide the you are in over your head and reward you with a lower score to scare away the lenders.

Set rules for yourself and your family when it comes to borrowing. You can't really avoid a mortgage, but things such as car purchases and vacations should have rules. When buying a car, try to buy the whole thing cash. If that is not possible, aim to have at least a 15% down payment on the purchase price. If you can't even come up with that, maybe you need to wait or buy a cheaper car. Boats, snowmobiles, motorcycles: these are toys and you really should not borrow 100% of the purchase price to buy them. The same goes for vacations: don't borrow money to go on vacation. If you already did, don't borrow for the next vacation before you have paid off the previous one.

These borrowing rules suck and they are no fun, but they will put you on much better financial footing and help you avoid the kind of overspending that will lead to credit problems.

Learn To Budget

Budgeting is a pain in the rear, even for people who are doing great financially. It is boring and it is restrictive, it sucks the life blood right out of you. Reaching or exceeding your monthly allowance for restaurant meals in a week is not fun. And where do unexpected dentist expenses go? What about roof repairs?

In many years as a lender for a bank I have given out hundreds of booklets on budgeting and personally given advice on the subject. There is a psychological barrier that make budgets so difficult. Everyone thinks they need to be perfect and on budget all the time, and once you go over your budget in even the least important category you feel like you broke your perfect record. Once perfection has been tainted, the baby is thrown out with the bathwater and the habit of budgeting is abandoned. Maybe abandoning your budget reinforces your belief that budgets are hard and you are bad with money. You need to get past this and do your best to stick with it.

Budgets are like Bootcamps for fat kids. There is that sick feeling at first when your body is woken up to reality. Then there are all the steps that follow that you just keep on messing up on and never really getting perfect. Then there is the cheating every once in a while when you somehow manage to get your hands on a bag of chips. After it's all said and done, it was no fun, you didn't do everything perfectly, but you still walked away a little better or even much better than before.

The point of a budget is to put everything down on paper. How much money is coming in every month? How much money is going out. Is less money going out than coming in but you are still going further into debt? Then you either missed a few items or are not totally honest with yourself, you will need to start again. Just knowing how razor thin the margin is between how much is coming in and how much is going out, might stop you from buying that cookbook that you will never use. Sit down and do your budget and be brutally honest. You don't even need to consciously try to save money, you subconsciously start spending less .

Break your spending into different categories and decide how much you should spend on each category. Figure out the costs that you cannot change, such as rent or mortgage payments or car insurance. Then figure out what your discretionary spending is, these are the things that are wants and not needs. Those are the categories that you can save money on. Set a budget and try to hit it. Celebrate every time you decide not to spend money.

Whenever you are less than perfect with your budgeting, don't be too hard on yourself. The idea of your budget is for you to be aware of where your money is going, and of where it should be going. Even if you stick to the budget only 2% of the time, you're still better off than not having a budget at all and sticking to it 0% of the time. Every little bit counts.

Authorized users

If you don't have the credit to get a new credit card, or even to extend your current credit line, then your best choice may be to find someone you trust and ask them to become an authorized user on their card. While most people will likely balk at the idea, you may be able to pacify them by explaining that you don't need a copy of their card or have any intent on using it, simply being listed on the card is enough to improve your credit utilization rating. Not only that, but you will also get credit for the on-time payments that this other person makes as well.

Open a new account

Improving your credit utilization rate is one of the best ways to start rebuilding your credit. If your current credit card company won't increase your credit limit you may way to try applying for another credit card instead. If your credit is not so hot then your rates are going to be higher, but this won't matter as long as you don't plan on using the card in the first place. Remember, credit utilization rate is a combination of your total available lines of credit so this can be a good way to drop your current utilization rate substantially, especially if you won't be able to pay off what you currently owe for a significant period of time.

Keep in mind, however, that if you choose this route then you are only going to want to apply for one new card every couple of months, especially if you aren't sure if you are going to be approved, as too many hard credit inquiries will only cause your credit score to drop, even if you do end up with a better credit utilization rate as a result. Spreading out these requests will give the inquiries time to drop off naturally and will prevent you from looking desperate to potential lenders which can also make it more difficult to get a new card.

Increase your credit limit

If you aren't currently in a position to pay down your credit card balance, you can still improve your credit utilization rate by increasing your current credit limit. This is an easy way to improve your credit utilization rate without putting any more money out up front. If you do this, however, it is important that you don't take advantage of the increased credit line as if you find yourself up against the limit again you will be worse off than when you started. Only pursue this option if you have the willpower to avoid racking up extra charges, especially if you are already strapped when it comes to the payments you need to make each month; decreasing your credit utilization limit while also making more late payments is a lateral move at best.

Pay your credit card bills twice a month

If you have a credit card that you use on a regular basis, say for example because it offers you reward points, so much so that you max it out each month, it may actually be hurting your credit even though you pay it off in full at the end of each month. This may be the case due to the way the credit card company reports to the credit bureau; depending on when they report each month it could show that your credit utilization rate is close to 100 percent depending on what your credit line currently is, thus hurting your credit score. As such, paying off your credit card in two smaller chunks throughout the month can actually help boost your credit without costing you anything extra overall.

Chapter 7: How to Get out of Debt

Being in debt can hold you back from achieving financial success and happiness. Credit card debts, in particular, are high interest debts that can pose serious threats to your financial security if allowed to balloon to uncontrollable levels. If you are deeply in debt, you have to face the problem and figure out how you can settle your liabilities as quickly as possible. Work out a repayment plan and be firm on your resolve to get out of debt fast. Stay motivated by constantly reminding yourself of the rewards and benefits of being debt-free.

Here are good reasons why you should pay off your debts fast and stay debt-free for life:

1. Being debt-free means you have full control over your finances. You will no longer be at the mercy of your creditors.

2. You will have the money to send your kids to great schools, buy the car you want, or live comfortably in your dream house.

3. Being debt-free means you can use your income to enjoy the finer things in life.

4. Not having to worry about payment and payment due dates reduces anxiety and stress and helps you live a happier and healthier life.

5. By staying out of debt, you will have more money to save and invest for your retirement.

6. You will be in a better position to prepare for your children's future and deal with life's challenges.

    When you set your sights on higher goals, it becomes easier to make sacrifices for a few months or years in exchange for a lifetime of financial security and abundance.

Strategies to Get Out of Debt

How you will settle your debt will depend on your actual financial situation and preferences. Here are proven strategies you can consider when deciding on a payment plan:

1. Make a list of everything you owe. Write down the creditor's name, loan balance, interest rate, and minimum monthly payment required.

2. Sort your debts by amount and interest rate. This will help you assess what credit card debt(s) to prioritize. The most popular method is to put more payment into the debt account with the higher interest rate while paying the minimum amount on the rest of the loans. Once this debt is fully paid, you can continue to use the extra fund to pay off the next card on the list. Using this method can help you pay your debts faster.

3. Another popular strategy is to prioritize payment for the card(s) with the lowest balance while paying the rest of the creditors the minimum amount due. This strategy can be a powerful morale booster. After paying the first target debt in full, you can use the extra fund towards the payment of the card with the next lowest balance.

4. Negotiate with your creditors for a lower rate. If your credit standing is good, banks will likely agree to give you a lower rate instead of losing your account to another creditor. You can use the savings from the reduced interest rate to pay off your principal loan.

5. Consolidating your debts and doing a balance transfer at a significantly lower rate are other options you can consider to free yourself from debt and at the same time help you save on interest charges. You can do this by asking one of your existing creditors to absorb loan balances from your other cards. Another way to consolidate your loans is by opening a new

credit line with a new lender and transferring your loan balances to this new account.

6. Avoid borrowing money to pay your debts or minimum monthly payments. Your goal is to free yourself from debt as fast as possible.

7. Immediately after establishing your emergency fund, prioritize debt payment and use any extra cash, bonuses, or tax refunds to pay down your debts. You will save big on interest charges by using your unexpected funds to settle your debts faster.

8. Don't use your credit cards to purchase new items or pay for your household expenses just because you have managed to free a portion of your card balance.

9. Once you have paid off a credit card debt, have your account closed and cut your credit card. If you must maintain a credit card for contingencies while you're still in the process of building your emergency fund, just maintain one card and keep it in a place where you don't have easy access to it.

10. Don't use your home as guarantee for the payment of your credit card balances. Remember that credit cards are unsecured debts and are given to you on the basis of your credit scores. If you fail to pay, you risk losing your home.

11. You can negotiate with your creditors and banks directly. You don't have to hire the services of a debt settlement company or financial agents to arrange a balance transfer. Educate yourself on simple financial calculations and be able to compare banks' offers on your own.

12. Constantly visualize yourself as living the life of your dreams because you have finally conquered debt.

13. Finally, to pay off your debts faster, free off more funds by controlling your expenses and making more money.

Chapter 8: Avoid These Mistakes While Repairing Credit

For many people, a credit card is merely a convenient way to make transactions. However, few people realize that the little plastic card also has the ability to wreak havoc on their lives if not used carefully. Ultimately, misusing your credit account can destroy your credit scores and ultimately hamper your credit.

One way to prevent the damages that poorly handled credit can cause is to know about the mistakes that people commonly make and learn how to avoid them.

Paying just the minimum

Issuers of credit cards set a minimum amount that you should pay every billing period. Some people have the wrong notion that this is a godsend because it is so small compared to the total amount. They couldn't be more wrong.

Paying just the minimum amount on your credit card debt will not only increase the time it takes to pay off your balance, but it would also accrue more interest. In addition, your credit score would suffer because as your balance grows, your credit utilization grows as well and that has a negative effect on your credit score.

To avoid having to pay more in the long run, try to pay the total balance every billing cycle. Don't let it accrue interest.

Ignoring Your Billing Statement

If you don't check your credit card's billing statement often, the more likely it is that you'll risk missing payment or paying less than you should have for it to be considered on time.

In addition, ignoring your card's statement will cause you to miss some important announcements, such as an announcement to the changes on your credit card's terms.

Make it a habit to check your billing statement because it will often be your guide to know if there are any false activities on your account. Besides, doing so will help you keep your spending in check.

To make sure that the payments have been correctly applied to your account, or if the all the charges are accurate, always check your card's billing statement.

Failure to report a lost or stolen credit card immediately

The longer you take to file a report about your lost credit card, the longer the thief or the one who has gotten your card has to charge up your credit account.

If you immediately report your missing card before any false charges are made, the sooner you'll avoid possible responsibilities you have to deal with for the said charges. The sooner you report a missing credit card, the sooner it would limit your liabilities for false charges.

Canceling Your Credit Card

Now that you have finally paid off all your credit card bills which have been stressing you out for ages, your first impulse might be to get rid of your credit card as soon as possible, which is usually done by cutting up your card and closing your account.

But don't be too quick on doing that, as closing down your account so suddenly can actually lower your credit score. Keep in mind that the age of your accounts affects your credit scores.

Even if you have paid off your credit card, it would be much better for you if you just leave your credit account open, that is until you are 100% sure that you can offset the possible reduction in credit score by making changes that would boost it. Just keep it open and maintain low utilization.

Paying Late

Always pay for your monthly payments on time. If you keep on forgetting about your due dates, then you should come up with a system that can remind you about them. For example, you can set up auto pay with your bank or use apps to set reminders. If the primary reason is inconvenience, then organize your bills so you could schedule the best time to pay all if not most of them.

If you keep on paying late for your monthly payments, it can cost you for up to $38 in late fees, which will also depend on the number of times you have been late for the past 6 months.

Also, falling behind your payments for more than 30 days will also affect your credit score. But if your existing payment is more than 60 days late, then your card's issuer may raise your interest rate up to the penalty rate available.

Loaning your credit card

When you loan your credit card to another person, you will no longer have control over the purchases that they are about to make.

In the end, you'll still be responsible for paying all the bills, even if the person who borrowed your card doesn't pay you for the expenses.

Never ever loan your card to someone, even if it's someone you know, except if you are prepared to take responsibility to pay for the purchases that they are about to make.

Not Knowing Your Credit Card Terms

If you know how your credit card company handles the late payments, you'll be more likely to pay for your card's bill on time. After all, you'll know exactly how much they cost you.

Letting your card get charged-off

Acquiring a charge-off is one of the worst things that can happen to your credit card report and credit score. A charge-off will remain on your report for 7 years, and could significant affect your ability to get loans and credit cards several years in the future.

It would take about a total of 6 months of missed payments for you to be charged with a charge-off status. Before your card gets to that point, ensure your delinquent accounts are current.

Applying for too much credit

If you are on the checkout line and the cashier asked if you want to apply for a store credit card for the discount, do not accept it outright. You may love to have a discount on your purchases, but it is still a credit card. Remember that each time you apply for credit, an inquiry will show up on your credit report and will pull down your credit score a little. The discount you think you'll be getting might not be worth it.

Also, be careful about opening too many credit accounts if you plan on applying for big loans, such as mortgage, car loan, and others.

Maxing your card out

Utilizing more than 30% of your card's limit can be quite dangerous for your credit score. Also, by getting close to your credit's limit, it will put you at risk for fees that are over the limit, and even the penalty interest will increase your card's charges once you exceed your credit card's limit. Therefore, to have a manageable payment amount and healthy credit score, always maintain a good credit card balance.

Getting pressured into accepting new cards

Have you ever noticed that sometimes most of the letters in your mail are about new credit card offers? Or maybe you have encountered countless strangers who are calling you to pitch you one? Well, don't think that these are just your imagination, because they are not.

A lot of credit card companies send out millions or even billions of credit offers every year, but this doesn't mean that you have to accept all of their requests or listen to their sale pitches. You can freely choose to get out of the prescribed credit card offers and out of the credit card telemarketing lists.

You can also get out of the email and phone solicitations from the mortgages companies.

Sharing your credit card number with other people

Some credit card holders sometimes share their card's number to pay for a bill. But if someone calls, emails, or have mailed you with some requests and unsolicited personal information, such as your Social Security number or credit card number, never reveal it even if the person sounds legitimate or nice. These kinds of requests are part of financial scams that mostly target seniors. These fraudsters are trying to make unauthorized use of your good name and credit or steal your money.

If you do become a victim of identity theft, immediately report it to your Federal Trade Commission and to your local police department.

Paying tax bills with a credit card

If you don't pay for a federal tax debt, the IRS will have the power to tax your assets, put a right to claim or hold your property, or seize your tax refunds. However, none of it should intimidate you into paying them with your credit card.

The reason is that if you use your credit card, you will also have to pay for an interchange fee. This may run anywhere from 2% to 4% of the amount that you are paying for.

Now, add those to the 12% to 18% interest that you have to pay to your bank if you think of adding the tax charge to your balance. A better solution to your problem would be to set up a repayment plan with the IRS and pay your tax debts over time.

Applying for credit repair recklessly

If you have recently gone through a serious personal setback such as a foreclosure, divorce, or bankruptcy, your credit standing might be shaky or maybe even downright bad.

However, looking for a quick fix can actually put you in the hands of a con artist that specializes on tricking people i.e. charge you with hidden costs or high upfront fees for their fake services.

Also, be aware of companies or an individual that promises to "fix" your bad credit overnight. Fixing a really bad credit score won't happen overnight, it lasts for days, weeks, or maybe even a month if the process is slow.

Using your credit card to withdraw cash

Using credit cards to withdraw cash could be bad because the credit card issuer is not able to monitor the spending, and thus view it as a high-risk loan and subsequently charge higher interests.

If you don't fully pay off the amount you withdrew within a month, your balance will start racking up some interests. Therefore, you can quickly lose control over your debt if not handled as soon as possible, particularly if you only pay the minimum amount monthly.

Aiming for the "rewards"

We people have been known to use credit for all kinds of things, be it a lavish vacation or jewelry, or even cars and in some cases, expensive novelty products.

However, making large purchases on a credit card is definitely a no-no unless you are 100% sure that you can immediately pay off such large amounts in full.

Whatever benefits that you may gain, in terms of flier miles or hotel check-ins, will come with interest charges, which you'll have to pay if you don't immediately pay your balance off every month.

Ignoring Your Credit's Warning Signals

To improve your chances of getting a healthy credit rating, check your credit reports for free for at least once or twice a year from a government-mandated website. However, if you're in the process of building or rebuilding credit, that isn't just enough. Check it once a month. You may also want to sign up for credit monitoring services, among others.

Also take note of warning signs that indicate you might be in a debt trouble such as missing payments, only making minimum payments, regularly seeking for 0% card offers, a low-rate balance transfer just to afford payments, or charging without knowing how to pay for bills.

If any of the following warning signals are familiar to you, it's time you get your act together to start repairing your credit.

Financial Mistakes

Not building business credit

Many business owners are making big financial mistakes when it comes to business credit. One of the big mistakes is not building their business credit; they do not spend extra time and effort to build business and financial credibility for their business.

Not paying bills on time

Another major financial mistake business owners make is not paying their bills on time. In many cases, this lowers the business credit score, making it harder to get new credit at good terms.

Mixing personal and business credit

Another serious issue is the business owner mixing personal and business credit by using personal credit to pay for business debts. Investing personal credit and cash into the business is a big financial mistake. This may earn them trade credits, but those credits are not helpful in building business credit since they are not reported to the business credit reporting agencies.

Putting personal assets at risk to business debts

Using personal credit cards, cash, line of credit, etc. to pay business expenses creates a big financial issue as it puts the business owner's family assets at risk to business debts. When this happens, the business owner is creating personal liability by pledging personal assets rather than utilizing corporate credit

Most business owners do not manage their business credit, as they should, as an Asset rather than a Liability. A lot of business owners do not realize that business credit is an asset that grows with the business. A personal credit has a predetermined limit and borrowing ceiling, limiting what the business owner can be approved for. Building a strong business credit profile will help the business cash flow by reducing or improving vendor and supplier terms, credit card rates, financing costs and insurance premiums.

Chapter 9: How to Delete Bad Credit Legally

Public records that appear on your credit report include civil judgments, tax liens and bankruptcy filings.

Tax liens: the first thing you are going to want to do is to ensure that the debt has been paid in full. Next, you are going to want to go ahead and prepare to file a dispute. The federal government has a Fresh Start program that makes this process fairly straightforward. To qualify you are going to need to be current on your taxes and have received a Release of Tax Lien document. You will also need the original form that provided notice of the lien in the first place. You will then need to fill out IRS form 12277 Application for Withdrawal of Filed form 688Y, available at IRS.gov. You will then need to submit this, along with your original form and proof that you have paid off the lien to the IRS. You should then receive IRS form 10916(c) which states that the federal lien has been withdrawn. Finally, you will submit a copy of that form to the credit bureaus with a request that they remove the inaccurate information from your report.

Judgements: Having a judgement on your credit report can be nearly as harmful as having a repossession or a loan default. While removing a judgement is possible, it is not as easy as removing a late payment or a credit inquiry. A judgement shows up on your credit report if a judge signs off on a statement saying that you owe a specific debt. This occurs when a lawsuit is filed against you for the purpose of collecting a debt, even if you weren't aware of the court proceedings at the time. It is important to keep in mind that just because a judgement was issued against you, that doesn't mean the other party was paid, which is a fact that you will use to your advantage.

There are two different ways to deal with a judgement once it has hit your credit report, you can have the judgement dismissed, also known as vacated, or remove the judgment from your credit report.

Dismiss a judgement: In order to have a judgement dismissed, you need to file a motion to dismiss the judgment with the court that issued the judgement in the first place. This is essentially an appeal that states the original outcome was inaccurate or unfair based on a specific number of reasons. First you will want to look through the proceedings and ensure that the person who requested the judgement in the first place went ahead and followed all the correct procedures and laws for doing so in your area. If there was mismanagement of this process, the odds are that the judge didn't know about it when the judgement was made.

In addition to following up on the judgement process, you will need to ensure that the person filing the judgement also followed proper court proceedings as you may be able to win out based on a technicality. This is especially important if you failed to show up for your court date and the plaintiff won by default as long as you had a valid reason for not showing up for the hearing in the first place. Again, it is important to familiarize yourself with local laws for this process to be effective.

When you prepare your motion to vacate it is important you follow local rules for civil procedure to the letter, the rules for your area should spell out exactly what you need to do, explain valid reasons a judgment can be vacated and will often include specific language you will need to use to file your motion.

The document you create should explain why the judgement should be vacated, starting with the reasons why you are bringing the motion forward. You will need to state your procedural defense and explain why you missed the original hearing if that is what happened. Valid reasons include that you were not served properly, that you responded to the summons but there was no initial judgment or that you did not have time to make it to the hearing based on when you were served. There may be other valid reasons in your area as well.

You will also need to include reasons why the judgement would have been dismissed if you had been at the hearing including things like, the collection agency failed to respond to your validation request or that the debt amount exceed local usury interest limits.

Bankruptcy: Removing a bankruptcy from your credit report is the most difficult black mark to remove. While it is far from a sure thing, a general rule is that the older the bankruptcy is, the easier it is to remove. To get started you are going to want to look for errors relating to it, if there are then you are in luck. If you find errors you can go about asking the bureau to remove them in the standard way.

Regardless if the information is accurate or not, you are still going to want to ask the bureau to verify the bankruptcy as they will be unlikely to go about doing it in the right way. Assuming they come back and tell you that it has been verified by one court or another, this is almost always inaccurate as courts rarely verify bankruptcies. With this information in hand, you will want to reach out to the court that has been specified and ask them how they verify bankruptcies. You can call and ask for this information, typically from the clerk of the court. Assuming they explain that they don't verify bankruptcies you will then want to get that fact in writing.

When you receive this letter in the mail, you will then want to send it to the bureau that claimed to have verified your bankruptcy in the first place along with a letter explaining what it is and stating that, as the bankruptcy was not actually verified, you want it taken off your record as by not doing so previously, but saying that they did, they are in direct violation   of   the   FCRA.

Deletion of Negative Public Records (Judgments)

Ever had your wages garnished?

I did – I fought – I won

I had to pay a settlement, but I got the judgement VACATED from the clerk of court and removed completely from my credit record.

Garnishments are the worst thing for your credit, you don't want this on your report, and any potential employers will have a serious problem with this.

I used whatever leverage I could find and wrote a letter to the Judge that handled the case and explained in lengthy detail how it all happened, why the creditor was being too harsh and ruthless and what violations I believed the committed.

The Judge actually ruled in my favor for the second hearing which I could not attend due to work, I gave my letter to the bailiff before the court date.

I still had to pay court costs but I won. I wasn't even there, and the Creditor's attorney was very upset, apparently he losing the case really made him look bad to the firms' Partners.

Public Records will require serious measures to get vacated or deleted. Keep in mind anything is negotiable if you can find the leverage or violation within the Fair Credit Acts. Most of the time they are there, but you have to look very hard.

In addition, getting creditors to vacate or delete a public judgement can be accomplished with settlements and negotiations while leveraging the Fair Credit Acts. Where there is a will there is a way. Do you think attorneys give up when the odds are stacked against their case? No way, they find loopholes and any leverage they can find – I would suggest you view defending your credit report the same way, only the consumer laws are MORE biased for you.

Chapter 10: Right Mindset for Credit Management

Having the mindset of a lender allows you to manage your money in a way that makes you a good credit candidate in the eyes of lenders. Apply the following tips when handling your finances to help you develop the mindset of a lender.

1. Do your research.

Knowing how money works will go a long way toward helping you maintain your credit report's good standing. Keep your good credit score from dipping by reading books on finance management. It helps if you have knowledge on how your accounts and loans work so that handling them will be easier on you. When you take steps to understand how money works in general, you equip yourself with tools that will help you make wiser financial decisions and avoid a bad credit rating.

2. Confirm your closed accounts.

It doesn't matter if they are bank accounts, credit accounts, or even your utility company accounts – what does matter is that you ask for a written confirmation for every account you close. Make sure that each closed account has been fully paid up. It helps if you follow up with your bank or credit card company a couple of months afterwards to confirm that the accounts have been closed.

3. Know how lenders view you.

Your credit score is not the only thing that lenders will often examine in your credit report. They also take the time to look at other financial indicators such as your employment history, your income, and your savings. Work on keeping these details in order to help you maintain your good credit score and achieve good overall credit, especially since there are a number of lenders who employ their own methods of computing credit scores.

4. Constantly update your records, including your current address.

Making sure that all your records are updated regularly helps you keep your lenders and financial managers up-to-date as well. It helps to keep all of your financial information in one folder at home, including and especially your current address. It will serve as a reminder to contact your creditors in case you move and give them your new address. This will prevent the problems of not getting your bills, being unable to pay them, and seeing your credit score go down as a result.

5. Aim for stability.

As much as possible, do not move around too much. Moving frequently results in your having to switch banks. This prevents you from developing long-term relationships with any of them, and this has a negative effect on your credit score and credit report. On the same note, it helps to avoid changing jobs too often. To some lenders, frequent job changes is an indication that you are likely to make loan defaults or go off with the money without paying. It also helps to avoid frequently changing your credit accounts and credit companies. Doing so prevents you from building a good credit relationship with any of them and could cause you to have a low credit rating.

6. Keep the lines of credit communication open.

As soon as a problem in your finances crops up, take steps to talk to your creditors. This will give them reassurance about your being responsible as a borrower, and this helps to prevent your credit report from being negatively affected. All it takes is calling them over the phone and arranging to have your payment schedules adjusted, as well as getting your penalties waived free of charge.

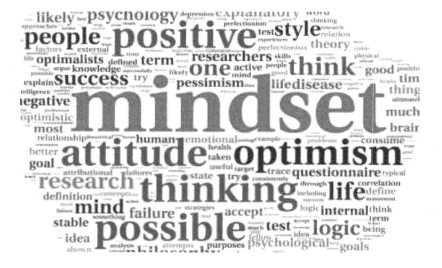

Chapter 11: Financial Freedom

Developing Wealth

Positive Wealth Consciousness

Throughout the years through a research study, interviews, I've discovered that individuals who have an excellent deal of wealth and individuals who preserve a favorable capital have actually established a favorable wealth awareness.

I keep in mind talking to a buddy, who owns a chain of hotels across the United States and is now expanding into Canada and overseas. He explained he had actually originated from an immigrant family; his daddy worked as an accounting professional and later on opened a store while his mother put herself through school eventually ending up being a nursing sister. However, my point is he didn't have a family that provided him with a million dollars to start his endeavor. Rather he began off working for his father, ultimately took control of the company, bought another, made it a success offered it and purchased another till he got his first hotel just outside Dallas.

Lets define positive wealth consciousness as a method of believing that you can and will generate income. It involves thinking that it is your right to generate income and create wealth. It needs that you concentrate on all the great things that your wealth can do for you and those around you. If you have wealth, you will assist more individuals, and it means understanding that. It suggests putting your ego aside- not wanting wealth so that you can flaunt and say: "Look at me, I'm rich." Rather it suggests saying: "Yes, I have a lot of wealth which enables me to take care of a lot of people, including my household and all those that I help when I invest my money."

You will invest your money, let's face it , the more you have, the more you will spend.

In order to bring in wealth, you need to very first take a look at where you are now and then create a realistic approach for a couple of months,a year, or more years. Perhaps you are indebted due to the task-

intending to have a million dollars in 6 months is not being extremely realistic. Rather your very first priority must be to get and get a job out of debt. If you currently have a job and you want to make more cash then offer yourself some sensible targets for the next 3 months, 6 months, year, and 5 years. Now I understand a few of you will say it's tough to generate the income, I do not know what to do to make more money, I'm in debt and don't understand how to go out. For each issue, there is an option of solution otherwise, we would not have problems. Concentrate on finding an option. Train your mind to focus on the service. Begin to forward messages to your conscious mind for a solution. Do this frequently, and you'll get answers. The money will not fall from the sky, but you will be guided to it. How Do You Train Your Mind? You initially focus on what you desire. Let's state you wish to find a task- you start to proclaim that you know what to do to find a task.

What You Can Do To Attract Wealth

There are a variety of techniques you can employ to attract wealth, regardless of your situation. You have to get your mind to work for you and not versus you. Here's a little exercise you can do. Get a notepad and a pen. Now begin thinking of generating income or enhancing your financial resources. Jot down all the thoughts that come to mind when you think of enhancing your finances or creating wealth. Be sincere – then you will see this list. Keep going until you feel you have had to satisfy. Keep contributing to that list throughout the day. Then when you feel you have got enough - have a look at what you wrote. Highlight the thoughts that are favorable and circle the ideas that are negative. How lots of are you negative? Any negative thought that you have about money or to improve your finances is connected to a belief that you have about money and only works against you. If you believe it's challenging to make more cash, you'll only have problems when it concerns making cash. Why? Due to the fact that your subconscious mind is just going to develop your truth based on your beliefs. If these beliefs are bad or great for you, it doesn't care. It simply acts upon your guidelines, and those guidelines are your beliefs and thoughts. To alter your thoughts and you change your beliefs. Modify your beliefs, and you change your life.

Chapter 12: The FUQ'S (Frequently Unasked Questions): Things Everyone Should Know About Their Credit Score.

Frequently Unasked Questions

In life, questions are more important than answers. The reason is that you get a clearer understanding of things when you learn to ask the right questions. So, I called this the Frequently Unasked Questions because this section deals with questions that people want to ask about but is not really what everybody asks, so they assume it is not necessary to know. Just like I have mentioned over and over again in this book, the best way to understand the credit score world is to never assume you know it all. Keep asking and researching, find out information about your credit report, credit score and how banks make use of your credit history in deciding on your loan requests. Here, I will show you questions you may already know the answers to, but I will take my time to properly explain them and also questions you might have never even thought of yet, but I bet you they will be useful in the long-run.

What is the catch in having a good score?

Everyone should be interested in having a good score as this has several advantages. Some of which are, for a case where you would like to take a loan out, it will help you get very favorable conditions. This also supports you in winning the contract for a new apartment. Many property managers do not take the risk and look for solvent tenants in particular who pay the rent on time. These are just a few benefits, amongst many.

What factors influence my credit rating?

When you're shopping, either online or in a fixed shop or supermarket, there's a lot to consider. "Zero percent financing" sounds like a good idea, but bear in mind that this is also a loan. This is not often concluded with the company, where a product is to be bought, but with a cooperating bank. Because "zero-percent financing" is a loan, it is only available to consumers with good credit ratings and has an impact on your score. Paying attention to some hidden costs such as processing fee which is also very important. Either it is online or on the ground, when ordering from mail-order companies, endeavor to pay invoices on time. Otherwise, your score can be affected negatively. A corresponding score means that you can't order on account.

What is the importance of performing scoring procedures?

The scoring procedures are performed most times when you want to borrow. Even if you're using the "zero-percent financing," a scoring is carried out nevertheless. Moreover, the scoring plays a major role if a company is to provide a service before you pay for it. This often happens with mobile phone contracts or shipping dealers a lot. However, the score value does not only determines whether a loan is granted to you but on what terms and conditions as well. A customer with a good score will obviously receive better terms and conditions than a customer with a bad one. They can, therefore, be able to ascertain that the customer will repay the credit without hitch or difficulty. This then means that scoring procedures help companies, banks and as well as service providers, in particular, to assess the risk of a business and be able to hedge it.

How do they compose my personal score?

The scoring process involves, on one part, one's personal data and historical experience on the other. From this, a phantom score is prepared by means of mathematical-statistical methods, allowing indications of the future behavior of the "scanned" person. Including the data and experience values, already included in the evaluation, the socio-demographic data (such as gender, age, the payment experience, known address, etc.) or contract data (such as the number of accounts and credit cards). However, the specific composition of scoring is a whole lot different for each scoring provider and is not made public.

Are credit rating and credit scoring the same?

No, they aren't. Score values deal with the creditworthiness of a group of people. However, the term "creditworthiness" or credit rating is known as the solvency of an individual or a company.

What does scoring entail?

Scoring helps to predict the behavior of groups of people with similar characteristics. Mathematical-statistical methods are used to calculate scores of a group of people and hence a statement is obtained on the risk of payment default of those people. The assumption most times is that people with the same characteristics will also tend to behave the same manner. Hence, this suggests that scores do not evaluate the creditworthiness of a single person, but rather predicts the payment behaviors of a group of people to which a specific person belongs to. In the scoring process, empirical values from the past are applied to make deductions on similar events that play out in the future.

What time was credit scoring born?

Around the late 1950s and early 1960s, banks in the United States of America started working together by sharing their customer data, which included account balances and payment histories especially.

This method was, at first, limited to just small communities.

However, as of the 1970s, several large companies emerged as leaders in credit reporting.

In 1970, the American Congress initially approved the Fair Credit Reporting Act (FCRA) in order to control the manner in which credit verification companies handled personal consumer information. This was the first step towards the regulation of the sector.

In the early 1980s, loans, requests, detailed personal information (including social security numbers, addresses, date of birth) and also payments that are still the basis of the credit valuation was electronically stored.

Why credit scoring? Why does it exist?

The credit history reporting system aids banks in not lending money to customers who have already been over-exposed and tagged as bad payers.

Until less than 80 years ago, the banking sector was a different experience entirely. Then, if you want to borrow money, you had to go into a bank branch and convince a manager one-on-one to grant you a loan. A proof of your income would have been requested from you as well as personal references who could guarantee your reliability. Back then, most loans were taken care of by guarantees, meaning that good collateral had to be offered to pay off the loan.

The commonest example of a loan guaranteed today is the loan for buying a property. In this agreement, the property is still the one that acts as the collateral.

With time, the high availability of credit cards as a comfortable electronic purchasing tool has also cleared the unsecured loan. And even if the unsecured loan were more profitable to banks, it was still very risky because there would be no guarantee for the bank to repay the sum paid if the debtor does not repay the loan.

Because of this, the credit scoring system came into play and was created to enable banks to have a central source of information on prospective customers.

What are the other factors that influence your credit scoring?

Yes, some of which are the average age of your current accounts, recent funding requests and any collateral that has been pledged against your assets.

Each of these makes up about 10-15% of your credit score.

The longer you have the current account, the better. Also, try to limit the credit requests to no more than two at least every six months. When you have too many credit requests in a short time, it can decrease your credit score as it suggests that you are in desperate need of money.

However, there is an exception for those whose credit requests are of the same nature. This will indicate that you are making an evaluation of a particular expense.

If it happens that these requests occur within a month or so, it will be generally accepted as one request.

What does the personal information in my credit scoring consist of exactly?

Your credit scoring contains all information about you, which includes your name, social security number, address and information about your financial assets, such as payments histories, balances and loan applications.

Your credit report majorly contains detailed information on recent activity on your financial accounts. This includes:

Credit requests: whenever you request a credit, either you have been approved or not.

Open loans: the data will have the bank, the loan amount, the loan opening date, the monthly payment amount and the payment history.

Use of credit cards: data includes the ban, credit limit, account opening date, payment history and the monthly payment amount.

Closed accounts: a closed account remains on the report for a maximum of up to seven years.

Public accounts: include judicial decisions and bankruptcy declarations.

How do you know you are doing a good job? How do you measure your progress?

As much as your credit report contains all information about your credit history, your credit score remains the best way to measure your progress in building your credit. Your credit score is referred to as the numerical summary of all information contained in your credit report within a particular time. It is the number that lenders and creditors use to decide whether to approve your requests and what interest rate to charge.

There are sites on which you can get your scores free of charge, some of which are creditkarma.com and creditsesame.com. You can also get your for FICO number for an affordable fee at myFICO.com. This FICO score, especially, is the one most creditors use.

This way, you can regularly monitor your credit score and update yourself on the changes that occur over time in your credit history.

How can I repair my bad credit scoring?

It's the same method for building a good one! Paying bills on time and staying away from debts. The best way to repair your credit is to pay your bills, reduce the level of debt per time and limit demand for fresh loans.

It would take about one or two years of responsible credit management to see your credit score improve exponentially. There are no shortcuts. Stick with this and you will see the change you desire

Chapter 13: Business Credit Cards

Whenever you attempt to open up a new business, you will need some funding to cover a lot of its initial expenses. Your personal credit card will be sufficient to start the business but only to a point. If the business you are planning to set up is of a certain size, you might want to apply for a business credit card.

What are business credit cards and what makes them different?

A business credit card shares mostly the same functions with a typical personal credit card. You use them to make transactions and pay for the charges each card makes at the end of the month. However, there are certain aspects that make a business credit card considerably different from your typical card.

1. It's Not Covered by Most Consumer Protection Laws

This is quite simple: under the law, businesses are of a different category from what you will call "consumers". Sure, you can tell yourself that you yourself are a consumer but the credit card was issued for the legal entity that makes up your business.

This means that certain consumer protection laws like the Credit Card Act of 2009 won't apply to you as the card holder. This could lead to a number of problems which will include sudden shifts in that card's Annual Percentage Rate, even overnight at some instances, and charges for penalties and fees that border on being expensive and unreasonable. However, there is a silver lining to all of this. If your business is quite small, some consumer protection laws might be extended to you. This is not true for all issuers so it's best not to expect to be covered once you are issued the card.

2. Higher Credit Limits

Due to the fact that your business is going to make a lot of expenses, the starting credit limit for a business credit card tends to be higher compared to personal ones. As such, if you can expect your business to make a lot of notable transactions, it's best that you apply for a credit card for businesses so you don't max your cards out quickly.

Of course, the same things that affect your credit score as a private individual will also affect you as the business owner. Even with the higher credit limit, the system of credit utilization rates still apply. Any credit you have available on that card, then, will be compared to the credit that you actually use on a regular basis. Depending on the reporting agency, credit utilization may comprise 30% to 40% of your score.

If you are not the type to overly rely on your business credit card, this could be an advantage for you. The higher credit limit means that it will take several huge purchases for you to even reach the 30% threshold reporting agencies recommend credit card users stick to. So as long as your credit utilization is within 15% to 19%, your credit score should remain high.

3. It Affects All Credit, Both Business and Personal

When it comes to being a business owner, the distinction between your personal credit and the business's credit is often blurred. In other words, your personal credit can affect how the business itself can apply for and use credit.

For instance, when issuers look at your application for a business credit card, they would look at your personal information and check if you have what it takes to handle the kind of liabilities that their product entails. As such, poor financial management skills might affect your ability to secure a credit card for the business in the first place.

It also goes without saying that reporting your transactions to the reporting agencies can get mixed. For instance, you might get a credit report where your entries for both your personal and business transactions are made into your timeline. Of course, this means that any mark reported to that agency regarding your business credit card's transactions, whether good or bad, will affect your credit score.

4. Perks

Due to the fact that business cards are a bit more demanding to maintain, certain credit card issuers offer certain perks for those that do apply for such. The most common perks are discounts for payments of several utility services like electricity, Internet connection, and phone connection. Some issuers even provide discounts on Wi-Fi rates as well as office supplies which might be an advantage for businesses that rely a lot on these.

However, you might be more interested with flat-rate rewards programs where you can avail of certain bonuses every time you make a purchase with the card. It's best to consult with the issuer first before you submit your application so you know what rewards you can expect if you frequently use that card.

Personal vs. business: Which card should you choose?

As was stated, there is the option to use your personal credit card over a business credit card for most of your transactions. If you are still deciding whether to stick to your personal card or apply for a business card, there are certain factors that you should consider.

You might be better off with a business credit card if:

• You are a starting entrepreneur who wants to build your business's credit trustworthiness.

• You run a company whose expenses require a larger credit limit.

- Your expenses align most with reward categories that business cards offer.

- You no longer want to deal with low credit limits.

Who can apply for a business credit card?

Naturally, the first requirement you need to qualify for a business card is to have a business. So, if you don't have at least any form of business, does that mean that you are not qualified for a business credit card?

The answer, surprisingly, is no. You can actually qualify for a business credit card even if you are just interested in the rewards that these cards have.

The reason for this is quite simple: there is no strict definition as to what a "business" actually is. It could range from hawking wares at a flea market or running a corporation with a hundred employees in it. It doesn't even matter if your previous business experience involves setting up a lemonade stand outside your home.

So as long as the money you generated from your activities can be considered as business revenue, then you might find some use for a business credit card. Either way, the issuer will still look at your personal credit information to see if you have what it takes to meet the demands that the card entails.

However, a personal credit card might be for you if:

- You run a sole proprietorship whose business expenses fall below the usual personal credit card limits.

- Your expenses do not align with the rewards program most business credit cards offer.

- You are not interested in building credit for the business.

- You are not the one who would apply for a business loan anytime in the future.

Types of Business Cards

There are several business cards that you can apply for. They have the same functions and requirements but they will carry certain features that make them ideal in a number of situations. They are as follows:

1. Business Credit Cards

These are your typical credit card and they function mostly the same with a personal card. They have a credit limit that dictates how much you can use the card every month as well as how much you pay.

Whenever your card makes a charge, you are obligated to pay the charge each billing cycle. This doesn't mean you have to immediately pay the amount in full as you can pay in installments. Although, this does mean that you carry the balance month for month i.e. you will have to deal with interest rates until that debt is settled.

However, this does allow for a small financial cushion that small business owners can depend on during tough times.

2. Secure Business Cards

This card is ideal for businesses with little personal credit or none at all. Think of it as a credit builder card, only for business owners.

How it works is quite simple. When you apply for this card, you are required to deposit a minimum amount. This could be in between $2,000.00 and $5,000.00, depending on the card and the issuer.

This amount serves as your credit line and you can use that to pay for anything related to the business. Either way, every payment for that balance will be reported by the issuer to the credit reporting agency.

This way, your business can build up on its credit within a year. However, it's important to note that only on-time payments will be reported. Any payment you miss will be a derogatory mark, defeating the purpose of the card.

3. Business Charge Cards

Like the typical business card, charge cards have the same function as personal credit cards. However, they differ greatly in the aspect of credit limits since, basically, there is none.

Charge cards have something that is called as a "shadow" limit which tend to be higher than most credit card limits and can be flexible depending on the card holder's needs. They can also change depending on how often you use your card as well as the overall status of your credit history.

However, there is a catch: Going over the limit can cause your account to be frozen. Also, you can never carry your balance on a month to month basis. You'll have to pay the charge in full every billing period.

This card is recommended only for people who have full control over their spending habits. If you can spend only on what you can afford, this charge card might be ideal for you.

How to get a business credit card

The process of securing your business's credit card is surprisingly easy. In fact, the process is quite similar to getting a personal credit card. However, there are differences in the details that you will submit to the issuing company. Since this is a business credit card, then it would be apparent that the issuer would ask information regarding your business. The application form will include questions like:

- The legal name of the business

- Address

- The type of industry it belongs to. Some industries are considered high-risk and high-maintenance which could affect the approval of your application.

- The structure of the company whether you are a sole proprietorship, a partnership, or a corporation.

- The age of the business i.e. how long it has been operating.

- Number of people employed as well as the organizational structure.

- Annual revenue

- Estimated monthly expenditures and other finance-related matters.

It really depends on the institution as to what kind of information that they want from you. To make it easier on your part, it's best to look for the information on your part and prepare your documents and answers beforehand.

What you need to secure a quick approval

In the end, it is up to the discretion of the bank or any similar financial institution to decide whether or not to approve your application for a business credit card. To make them easily decide for your approval, there are a few things you have to do beforehand:

1. Have a Good to Excellent Personal Credit Score

Your personal credit score will actually influence how your application is going to be treated. That lender would have to make sure that you as the applicant have what it takes to meet the demands of the card.

For this, they would pull up a hard search on your personal credit history and look for any mark made regarding your financial activities. What one creditor would look for is different from another but it's safe to say that applicants with a history of on-time payments, good credit utilization rates, and minimal to no derogatory marks tend to have a better chance of getting their applications approved.

2. Have a Business

Although you don't exactly have to have a business to qualify for a business credit card, having one does tend to improve your odds of successfully securing one. The lending institution would most likely want to make sure that whatever credit or money you can secure through the card would be used to invest for an actual venture. One proof that you have a business is through securing an Employer's Identification Number from the Internal Revenue Service as well as opening a business account.

What transactions could the business credit card be used for?

There is actually no hard and fast rule as to where and how you should use your business's credit card. It has the same functions as your typical credit card albeit with a larger credit limit and a few more restrictions/obligations on your part.

The question, then, is not on where your business credit card will be the most applicable but on how to optimize its usage while minimizing the risks it entails. To do those, here are a few tips to keep in mind.

1. Set Limits

The 30% rule for personal credit card utilization rates apply here as well. If possible, do not go beyond 30% of the available credit when using the card. If the limit is at $10,000.00, then your spending should not be over $3,000.00.

Of course, there is a chance when the policy you have set up would not work in all situations. Some authorized users for the card might have different purposes in mind for it. This is where a bit of creativity comes into play.

You might set different limits for each user but you must set other limiters as well. For example, one user might only access the card for a certain set of situations or you rotate possession of the card to the different users on a bi-weekly basis. The point is to make sure that nobody gets to use the card for too long to avoid abuses.

2. Keep Everything Strictly Within Business

Even if you are running a sole proprietorship, resist any urge to use that card to spend for personal concerns. Keeping your business expenses separate from your personal one is one way to keep track of your expenses and claim deductions when taxing season comes around.

If you authorize your employees to use the card also, give guidelines as to what will qualify as a business expense. Having a system set up where employees have to seek approval before using the card and furnish receipts is a good way of enforcing accountability and limiting the card's use.

3. Make a Policy

If you are running a corporation, chances are your partners will also want to have access to that card. This would be an opportunity for you to draft a policy on how to use that card.

Make it a point to show to everyone that the card is accessible but only if they meet certain conditions and follow the guidelines. The point here is to be as transparent as possible in telling your staff and your partners who can use the card and for what purposes.

Chapter 14: Nine Steps to Credit Repair

Repairing your credit takes nine steps, each of which will be discussed in greater detail in the next few pages.

1. Obtain a copy of your credit report from the three major credit bureaus (Experian, Trans Union Corp., and Equifax).

2. Highlight all negative items.

3. Challenge each of the negative items.

4. Request an updated credit report; check to ensure that some of the negative items were removed.

5. Repeat steps 2-4 once every two months until no additional items are removed.

6. Prepare a consumer statement disputing each of the remaining negative items, and request that the Credit Bureau include the statement in your credit file.

7. Request that each Credit Bureau furnish you with the names and addresses of each creditor still reporting a negative entry for your account.

8. Contact each of these creditors and attempt to negotiate a settlement.

9. Request that updated copies of your credit report be sent to anybody who received your credit report in the past six months.

These steps are all based on the rights granted to consumers through the Fair Credit Reporting Act (FRCA). As you implement the steps outlined above do note that the FCRA will not protect any request, challenge, or consumer statement that can be proven to be frivolous in nature.

It is highly unlikely that this charge will be made by a creditor or credit bureau, as they know that your defense can be that you were simply acting according to your understanding of your rights as granted by the FCRA.

Step One: Get a Copy of Your Credit Report

Before you can start to fix your credit report, you must first figure out what it contains. If you still have your credit reports that I suggested you get at the beginning of this book, go to step 2. If you don't have a copy of your report, then do the following:

Contact the three major credit bureaus, Experian Inc., Trans Union Corp., and Equifax Inc., to see which agency has a file on you. You might also want to contact other local credit bureaus, because there may be several different versions of your credit report floating around. It is a good idea to start with the three major credit bureaus and deal with others later.

Although you may save $8.00, in your effort to repair your credit, you don't need any unnecessary credit denials added to your credit report at this time. This is the exact kind of information that you are trying to erase from your file. However, if you don't have the $24.00 necessary to buy all three copies of your credit reports, this is an option.

There are other ways of learning about your credit report. Instead of the letter request, you can call the Credit Bureau and make an appointment to review your credit file in person. It is advisable that you wait for the Credit Bureau to tell you everything they know about your credit history before you volunteer any potentially damaging information to other parties.

Step Two: Note All Negative Items on the Report

Each Credit Bureau has their own way of organizing their credit reports. Make sure that you read and understand all the information they send on how to read their report. It is up to you to determine which entries are damaging.

Such items may include a different social security number, incorrect name or spelling of your name, wrong addresses, and excessive number of inquiries, charge offs, late payments, judgments, or anything else that will keep you from being granted new credit.

Perhaps your record was confused with another customer who has a similar name or social security number. Maybe the negative information is outdated, beyond the seven year legal reporting limit imposed by the FCRA.

Step Three: Challenge Each of the Negative Items

Send letters to each Credit Bureau, challenging each of the negative items on your report, even though they may be true.The Fair Credit Reporting Act (FRCA) states that any credit item that is challenged by a consumer must be proven by the creditor in order to be considered verified.

If this re-verification is not completed in a timely manner (approximately 30 days) or if the challenge goes unanswered, the affected negative credit items must be completely deleted from your file, never to reappear.

Note: Do not challenge more than four items at a time. Challenging more than four may cause the Credit Bureau to deem your challenge frivolous and deny your challenge.

Your challenges can be based on the argument that:

You never made late payments to that account

The account is not yours

You don't remember the facts as stated on your credit report

You don't remember applying for the credit card

There may be other arguments applicable to your particular situation. The challenging process works very well because there are many factors working to your benefit:

Certain negative items cannot be proven because they were legitimately in error and should have never been reported in the first place

Credit denials are often thrown out by creditors soon after they are received. As such, these items are generally not reconfirmed. Also, if the item is over two years old, there is a good chance that these records are not retained by the creditor.

If you have already paid off the account, the creditor will probably not want to be bothered and will not respond to the challenge.

A creditor might not respond within the time constraints set by the credit bureau in accordance with the FCRA's guidelines, generally about 30 days.

There is also the element of human error that can come into play (i.e. they may lose the challenge report, can't find the proof, things get lost in the mail, etc.) and result in a non-response by the creditor. The end result: the items are removed from your report. So, the odds are in your favor.

Step Four: Receive an Updated Credit Report

Within one month of challenging any negative items, you should receive an updated copy of your credit report (hopefully without some of the old negative items). If you have not received your new report within 6 weeks, call the credit bureau and remind them that you are waiting for the new copy of your credit report.

Step Five: Repeat this Procedure Once Every Two Months

Keep repeating steps 2 through 4 every two months until no additional items are removed as a result of your challenges. If the remaining creditors are determined to reconfirm their claims and continue to do so over and over again, it is time to move on to the next step.

Step Six: Prepare a Consumer Statement

Prepare a 100-word statement of dispute for each of the remaining negative items, and have the Credit Bureau include these statements in your credit file. These statements will show that the situation is still in dispute, and that there is another side to the story. You won't be declared unworthy of credit based on these claims, because they are still pending.

Step Seven: Request the Names and Addresses of Each Creditor

Explain to the Credit Bureau that there are still many mistakes on your credit report and that you would like to contact the creditors in question directly. Request that the Bureau send you the names, addresses, and phone numbers of each creditor still reporting a negative entry for your account.

Step Eight: Contact Each Creditor and Negotiate a Settlement

Negotiations between each creditor may differ depending on the circumstances. Creditors of unsecured loans are motivated to settle because after a certain amount of time these accounts are written off as a total loss; any payments would be considered to be "found" money, so you will probably have a very willing negotiating partner.

Step Nine: Ask That They Send Out Your Updated Credit Report

When your credit report is as clean as it's going to get, contact each Credit Bureau one more time. Request that updated copies of your credit report, be sent to all the creditors who received a copy of your credit report within the past six months.

Chapter 15: Appraise Your Current Financial Status

Now since you have decided to learn to manage your personal finances, let us start by appraising your current financial status. There are few questions you must ask yourself to know the equilibrium of your income and expenditure. Answer the following questions –

- Do you often encounter paucity of money for your daily expenses?
- Do you eat frequently out, thus spending a lot of money?
- Do you live paycheck to paycheck?
- Are you at the loss of words when asked how much is your household/personal expenses?
- Do you despise or dread sudden domestic expenditure?
- Have you ever planned your monthly budget?
- Do you save money for a longer or shorter perspective?

If there are more than 4 No as the answer to this questionnaire, your income and expenditure are not balanced and need immediate attention.

Scrutinizing Income vs. Expenses

It is vital to monitor our income and expenses and keep them in tandem. Any disparity in maintaining their equilibrium will result either in debts that would only be mounting and multiplying gradually. Spendthrift people often spend rashly and later on suffer financial setbacks that are often irreparable. Moreover, strict monitoring and streamlining of income and expenditure is going to render long-term benefits that would be felt in later stages of life.

Here are some genuine and practical tips to monitor our incomes and expenditures thus to make the most of our monetary funds -

Watch where you are Spending

It is a good money managing strategy to know your expenses to the maximum extent. There may be some unforeseen expenses that may rock your budget, but enough scope should be there in your monthly budget to accommodate them. Include all sorts of expenditures you come across in your day to day life starting from your groceries to your evening drinks. When the entire list of expenditure is going to be on paper, you will realize how much money is spent uselessly on frivolous things.

Cut down the Unnecessary Spending

Now once you have complete and comprehensive list of expenses with you, you know where you income would be going. Trust me; you will have an impulsive feeling to cut short many worthless expenses that may deem to you simply useless. And this very is the objective of listing all your expenses. You can also bifurcate them into categories like – important, less important and least important, etc. The idea is to sift the expenses that you can do without.

Do Not Overindulge

If you have good and steady income, it doesn't mean that all has to be spent and splurged. Spare money is to be saved and sorted so they can be used when the need may arise. For example, if the income is 2000 USD, do not make a budget of that whole amount. Save some money aside and do not count that for the purpose of spending.

Spend Wisely

Wise spending can't be learned or implemented in a single day. It is not a procedure, rather a habit that has to be developed over the time. One can't be a wise spender one particular month and then start splurging the next. Get into a habit of watching your money and then think practical while spending. Wise money management does not lay stress on being a miser or a money-stasher. It teaches how to be a smart spender so that the worth of every penny is derived out. Start in a small way – like cutting the bills of fast food snacks that tend to be heavy on health, as well as pocket. Instead of this, buy lots of fruits and keep them stocked at home. This will benefit your reckless spending as well as your health.

Escalate your income

Smart spenders and savers are always on the lookout of the chances and avenues that would help them in multiplying their income. If you are a school teacher, start taking tuitions in free time. If you are a chef, start taking cooking classes during the weekend. The idea is to augment the inflow of money via multiple streams. A small effort from your side will open many avenues for bettering your income.

Carry Debit/credit card instead of cash

Do not carry the lot of cash in your pocket else you would be spending the lot of it. Though there are people, who tend to spend more when they have their debit or credit cards in their pockets. Just follow a viable routine that would prevent you from spending recklessly.

Ways to Monitor Your Expenses

There are plenty of ideas, tools and applications that can be used for keeping a track of our incomes and expenditures. You just need to have the intention of using these, and they would take care of the rest of the things. Some of them are -

- **Mobile Phone App** – The latest smart phones come with one or the other kinds of applications that help in keeping the record of monthly income and expenditures.

- **Money Box** – Keep a money box handy in your home and use it to store all the receipts and bill that you pay. This will keep clarity of all expenditures. Also, keep in the box a piece of paper that has the record of income.

- **Calculator** – There are specific budgetary calculators that help in maintain the record of expense

- **Diary/Note-book** - Maintain a small pocket diary or a notebook in which you can jot whatever you spend. You would know exactly what have you spent on daily, weekly, fortnightly or monthly basis.

Get Rid of Bad Debt

Debts are the most irksome factor that disturbs management of our personal finances. However, debts are not always bad. Interestingly, some of them are good also. The present economic scenario is making it sensible to pay for some of our purchases on credit so that one can make maximum use of their liquid cash. The credit taken will keep the factor of depreciation of money well in control with the help of the rate of interest.

The good debt must never be considered as a liability. It is rather an investment that tends to make our money grow over a longer period, giving us the chance to make optimal use of liquid cash. One apt example of good debt is education loan that is taken to pay for college or higher education. Taking an education loan doesn't always mean that the borrower cannot afford paying the fee in cash. This loan is also taken in order to take advantage of low-interest rate of education loan. Students avoid using the cash of their parents and start repaying their education loan soon after they complete their education and are ready to earn lucrative salaries. A mortgage is also considered to be a good debt as it is considered to be the money saver in the longer run. One can take help of mortgages for buying homes. This kind of debt comes with measly monthly payments while the liquid cash in hand can be used for some other purpose. Good debt is considered to be good for the fact that they come accompanied with the low rate of interest.

In contrast to good debts, bad debts are taken to buy those things or services that lose their worth fast and do not create any promising income in the long term. They also come accompanied with the higher rate of interest. One common example of bad debt is credit card debt that is known for creating a vicious circle of financial liabilities. Buying flashy and branded luxuries through your credit card and then feeling helpless over its non-payment for years to come is a classic example of bad debt. Other types of bad debts are cash advance loan and payday loan that charge astronomical rate of interests that get compounded if not paid on time. These kinds of loans are devised to take advantage of borrower's pathetic and helpless financial condition.

Don't allow accumulation of Bad Debt

Just like a debt can't be accumulated in a single day, it can't be resolved in on a distinct date. The primary requisite to manage our personal finances is to keep away from debts. If you already have few of them to irk you, start planning strategically.

Read below-listed suggestions that would make you wiser and judicious in developing money-saving habits –

Shun debt accumulation

If you are already debt-ridden, just stop there. Do not add more to your already loaded financial burdens. You ought to concentrate over resolving past financial liabilities, thus keep your further track clean and clear. There is no point in clearing one debt by taking two more. This way, your financial status is going to become murkier.

Don't Rely on Credit cards

Credit cards are the biggest reason and cause of bad debts. This financial product gives ready cash to spenders and makes them reckless and mindless spenders. Just keep them away and learn to live without them. Using a credit card simply makes for uncontrolled spending that leads to the further financial mess. Never close the credit card accounts until all debts against it are repaid back lest the credit score will get affected.

Develop sensible attitude

Debt accumulation does not happen out of need but out of lax attitude towards money. This calls for immediate change in attitude so that what causes debt can be cured. A strong will to develop a frugal and a judicious attitude towards money will certainly take care of many financial issues that are known to be caused due to irresponsible mind-set towards.

Alter your spending tendencies

Are you a mindless spender who buys not out of need but out of greed? If you are one such person who cannot restrain buying things that are not even needed, you need to cure yourself. Do not remain lounged in front of TV watching advertisements and ordering things online. Watching online shopping sites just as a hobby is a sure shot recipe for landing in debts. Buying just to look 'cool' in your friend circle will be financially suicidal.

Don't Allow Consumerism to overshadow your lifestyle

Since we live in the times of consumerism, we have started believing that there are many things that are simply indispensable for our subsistence. This is a wrong approach as we are the ones who are responsible for expanding our wants....mistaking them for needs. To ourselves debt-free we must trim our lifestyle and live in a thrifty way.

Add volume to your income

While cost cutting is always suggested for getting rid of debts, opening, multiple income channels will speed up the process. Better the income, more rapidly you would be able to shrug off your financial responsibilities. And moreover, earning extra is never going to hurt you in anyway. Income can be increased by doing any such thing that interests you. It could be either some money-making hobby of yours (like teaching cooking, music, dance or aerobics) or some skill (being a singer, writer or carpenter, etc.). Having an alternative income channel will cushion your financial crises.

Make timely payments for avoiding penalties

Understand that you are already in debt and paying extra and superfluous charges (that can be certainly avoided) will sap up your resources. Do not delay paying bills, do not jump traffic rules, do not drive while drunk as these are some of the cases where a lot of money get drained due to sheer negligence and carelessness. Some other ways to save precious money are –

- Withdrawing money from bank instead ATM

- Avoiding online booking of tickets

- Buying credit card after negotiating rate of interest

- Consolidating multiple loans into one single loan that has lower rate of interest

Making Budget and Abiding by It

Having a budget for your income and expenditure will help in streamlining your finances that are already ailing due to debts. Categorize your expenses and tweak them to fulfill all liabilities as and when required. You will start having a fair idea where and how much to spend, giving you complete control over your money matters.

609 LETTER TEMPLATES

Dealing with the Bureaus to Fix Your Credit Score by

Having Everything You Need to Know Explained in Detail

[LUCAS ANDERSON]

Legal & Disclaimer

The information contained in this book and its contents is not designed to replace or take the place of any form of medical or professional advice; and is not meant to replace the need for independent medical, financial, legal or other professional advice or services, as may be required. The content and information in this book has been provided for educational and entertainment purposes only. The content and information contained in this book has been compiled from sources deemed reliable, and it is accurate to the best of the Author's knowledge, information and belief. However, the Author cannot guarantee its accuracy and validity and cannot be held liable for any errors and/or omissions. Further, changes are periodically made to this book as and when needed. Where appropriate and/or necessary, you must consult a professional (including but not limited to your doctor, attorney, financial advisor or such other professional advisor) before using any of the suggested remedies, techniques, or information in this book.
Upon using the contents and information contained in this book, you agree to hold harmless the Author from and against any damages, costs, and expenses, including any legal fees potentially resulting from the application of any of the information provided by this book. This disclaimer applies to any loss, damages or injury caused by the use and application, whether directly or indirectly, of any advice or information presented, whether for breach of contract, tort, negligence, personal injury, criminal intent, or under any other cause of action. You agree to accept all risks of using the information presented inside this book.

You agree that by continuing to read this book, where appropriate and/or necessary, you shall consult a professional (including but not limited to your doctor, attorney, or financial advisor or such other advisor as needed) before using any of the suggested remedies, techniques, or information in this book.

Table of Contents

CHAPTER 1: Introduction

Basically, a 609 is known as a dispute letter, which you would send to your creditor if you saw you were overcharged or unfairly charged. Most people use a 609 message in order to get the information they feel they should have received. There are several reasons why some information might be kept from you. A 609 letter is sent after two main steps. First, you see that the dispute is on your credit report. Second, you have already filed and processed a debt validation letter. The basis of the message is that you will use it in order to take unfair charges off of your credit report, which will then increase your credit score.

When it is time to report your credit history at all, one of the credit bureaus is going to be responsible for including not only correct information but also the accuracy of the report. The use of this letter in credit repair is going to be based mostly on the idea of whether the credit bureau was responsible for how they verified the information they put onto the report, and if they can do it promptly. Credit bureaus are going to collect information on consumer credit from a lot of different sources like banks. Then they are going to be able to resell that information to any business who would like to evaluate the credit applications of the clients.

Credit bureaus are going to be governed by the FCRA or the Fair Credit Reporting Act, which is going to help detail what credit reporting agencies and information furnishers can and can't do when they decide to report information on the consumer. Using these 609 letters is the right way for us to clean up our credit a bit, and in some cases, it is going to make a perfect situation. However, we must remember that outside of some of the obvious benefits that we are going to discuss, and there are a few things that we need to be aware of ahead of time. Few limitations are going to come with this as well. For example, even after you work with the 609 letters, it is possible that the information will later be seen as accurate could be added to the report again, even after the removal. This is going to happen if the creditor, after the fact, can verify the accuracy. They may take it off for a bit if the 30 days have passed, and they are not able to confirm at that point. But if the information is accurate, remember that it could end up back on the report.

While some people think that it is possible, keep in mind that you are not able to eliminate any obligations to repay a legitimate debt. Even if you write out a 609 letter and you can get that debt removed from the credit report, whether that is for the short term or a longer-term, you still have to pay that legitimate debt. Do not use this to hide from your debts or get from paying them at all. Use this as a method that will help you to clear out some of the older options, or some of the debts that you have taken care of but remain on your reports. Besides, contrary to some of the myths that are out there when it comes to these 609 letters, the FCRA is not going to require that any of the credit agencies keep or provide signed contracts or proof of debts.

You can, however, ask them to give you a description of the procedure that they used to complete the investigation into your accounts. The FCRA, though, is going to give you as a consumer the right to go through and dispute some of the errors that show up on your credit report. This is not a way for you to go through and make some of your student loans or other debts go away, so you do not have to pay them any longer. But it is going to be one of the best ways that you can get information that is not accurately taken off the credit report. We can get a lot of things done when we work with the Section 609 letters, but they are not a magic pill that will make things disappear for us. They will make it easier for us to go through and get rid of information that is not correct and can ensure that we can get rid of debts that maybe we settled in the past but are still harming our credit. This is going to make it easier overall for us to ensure that we can get things organized and get a higher credit score that we are looking for.

How to File a Dispute with 609

It is important to note that there are several template letters for 609. What this means is that you can easily download and use one of these templates yourself. While you usually have to pay for them, there are some which are free. Of course, you will want to remember to include your information in the letter before you send it. You will want to make sure everything is done correctly as this will make it more likely that the information will come off and no one will place it back on your report again.

Make the Necessary Changes to the Letter

This will include changing the name and address. You will also want to make sure your phone number is included. Sometimes people include their email address, but this is not necessary. In fact, it is always safer to only include your home address or PO Box information. You will also want to make sure to edit the whole letter. If something does not match up to what you want to say in your letter, such as what you are trying to dispute on your credit report, you need to state this. These letters are quite generic, which means you need to add in your own information.

CHAPTER 2: What is Section 609 & How Does it Works

Section 609 refers to a section of the Equal Credit Reporting Act (FCRA) that addresses the right to request copies of your own credit reports and related information that appears in your credit reports. Strangely enough, Section 609 has nothing to do with the right to challenge facts about the credit reports or the duty of the credit-reporting agency to examine your disputes. There is no such "609 Conflict Letter" anywhere in the FCRA.

In fact, the FCRA contains a large amount of language that commemorates your rights to challenge the details found in your credit reports. It is, however, in Section 611 of the Legislation, rather than in Section 609. Thanks to section 611, we all have the right to challenge facts that we consider to be inaccurate or unverifiable. And if the information at issue cannot be checked or confirmed, it must be deleted.

Is the 609 Dispute Letter effective?

If you're searching for models for the conflicting text, there's probably a reason for that. Normally, customers send dispute letters to the major credit reporting agencies (Experian, TransUnion, and Equifax) because they feel that something about their credit report is wrong. This can happen if they have applied for a loan or other form of credit, and the lender has told them that they had been denied details on their credit report. It can also happen when they search for their credit report and discover accounts that they don't remember. The practical effect of the dispute letter is that it allows the credit-reporting agency to investigate and correct any reported mistake.

Although there is a lot of information available about 609 Dispute Letters, there is no proof that any particular letter template is more effective than any other letter template. And frankly, you should file your credit report dispute on the back of a beverage napkin and, whether it is legitimate, the details must be changed or deleted. The mode of distribution is essentially meaningless when it comes to your right to an accurate credit report.

Conversely, if the information on your credit reports is correct and verifiable, it is likely to stay on your credit reports. The style of your letter does not change that reality.

Credit scores can range anywhere from as low as 300 all the way up to 850 points. Where you fall on that spectrum can vary from one month to the next based on the information found in your report. Just like with your health, it is your responsibility to make sure that you take care of your credit and if you discover something is wrong, you must take steps to remedy it. To that end, you must know how to manage it properly. To be able to do that, you need to know just how the credit machine works.

You can Google credit repair services, and you'll probably find hundreds of them standing by, ready to take your money to help you get back on the right path. Unfortunately, many of these are scams and the few that are legit, are only telling you the most basic things to do. In many cases, these are things you can do yourself without outside help. Their main goal is to teach you how to fix the things that are wrong. What they don't do is help you to understand how credit really works and how to prevent yourself from falling into the bad credit trap again.

Understanding Your FICO Score

Almost every creditor will want to see your FICO score before he decides to give you credit. But knowing what the numbers really mean can make a huge difference in managing and taking back control of your financial future. As you gain more knowledge about how the system works, it can empower you. While other factors will weigh in the decision, anyone whose goal is to improve their creditworthiness needs to start with the FICO score as nearly all credit decisions will be based on it.

One of the first things you should understand is the scoring range so you can see what your number really means.

800+ is an exceptional score and is considered to be well above the average. Anyone in this range will find it very easy to get credit approval for just about anything they want. Sadly though, only about 1% of the population falls into this category.

740 – 799 is considered to be very good. While it is not the highest, it is still rated as above average. Anyone in this category will likely qualify for better interest rates and a wide range of credit privileges.

670 – 739 is considered to be good and is about average. They are not the optimum consumer, but they are considered to be in the "acceptable" range.

580 – 669 is considered a fair score. These consumers are usually below average and are labeled as subprime borrowers. This means that while they can get credit, it will be much more difficult for them; interest rates will be higher and they will often have to make higher payments for any purchases they make.

579 – 669 is considered to be a poor score. Consumers who fall in this range are often rejected outright in many places of business. However, they can get credit in altered forms. For example, they may be able to obtain a secured credit card, or they may be required to place a deposit to obtain the approval they need.

This is just a basic guideline of how the FICO score is broken down. Taking into consideration your payment history, the amount of debt you owe, and the type of credit you have will help to determine what your score really is.

It is important to remember, that your credit score does not remain the same throughout your life. Every month, your creditors are submitting new data about your payment activities to the credit bureaus so your score will constantly need adjusting. Also, there are other factors that the Fair Isaac Corporation also factors into your score that may not be as obvious. For example, your income or how long you've been on your job will have little bearing on your credit profile. Also, those who have new credit or a limited history will usually score much lower on the scale than someone who has a longer history of credit to report. This means a low credit score does not necessarily result from missed payments or even being in debt over your heads. Sometimes, it is the result of something entirely out of your control.

In the account history section, which will probably be the most detailed of the entire report, you will find the bulk of the information on you. It will look something like this:

- Creditor name: This could be the name of the merchant or creditor issuing the information.

- Account number: This would be the identifying number of your account. In many cases, this information will be encrypted to protect your privacy and to prevent someone from gaining access to your account information.

- Type of Account: This section will identify if it is a student loan, an auto loan, mortgage, or revolving account (like a credit card).

- Responsibility: Indicates whether you are the only person on the account or if other users are authorized to use it.

- Payment Record: Stipulates what the minimum required payment is on the account.

- Date opened: The exact date the account was established.

- Date reported: The last date the creditor submitted information to the credit bureau.

- Balance: the total amount owed on the account.
- Credit limit: What is the maximum amount of credit you can use.
- High balance or high credit: The highest amount of credit you have used on the account.
- Past due: Total amount of payments past due.
- Payment status: Is the account current, past due, or is it a charge-off (meaning that you haven't paid in a long time and the company does not expect that you will ever pay them).
- Payment history: Indicates how well you've been making payments since the account was opened.
- Collection accounts: This would include any accounts listed that have been sent to a collection agency.

Credit Inquiries

The report will also keep a record of how many times there has been an inquiry into your credit. A lot of inquiries with no new credit issued will reflect very negatively on your score. It is an indication that you have been trying to get credit but have received many rejections, this can make a creditor seriously reconsider taking a chance with you.

There are two different types of credit inquiries you should know about. The first is the "soft" inquiry, which are those made by lenders looking for promotional purposes. Perhaps credit card companies looking for new customers. The second, "hard" inquiries are those creditors that you have actually applied to. Perhaps a bank for credit cards, a department store, or a gas company.

Public Records

The public records section is where you will find information about anything legal in relation to your credit. If you've had a past bankruptcy, any court judgments, tax liens, or anything else it should be included here. However, this is not for everything related to your legal life only things related to your credit. If you've had criminal arrests or convictions, these are not a part of your report unless they have to do with your credit (passing bad checks to pay on your account, for example).

Ideally, you want to make sure that this section of your report is completely clear. Anything in this area will have a major impact on your score and can potentially keep you from getting any type of credit.

The good news is that even if you have a bad report, the negative records do not remain there indefinitely. Most information will remain on your report for 7-10 years. Inquiries will remain for two years max. That means that in time, these negative conditions will eventually drop off and as long as you can maintain a good record, your credit score will naturally improve.

The Fair Isaacs Corporation is very tight-lipped about the exact formula on how they actually calculate the scores, but at least you have a general idea of what they are looking for and what parts of your report need to be boosted to improve your total score.

How to Read Your Report

When you first receive your report, it will probably be a little confusing. Now that you know what each section actually shows though, it will be easier to decipher exactly what it says about you. However, you'll probably want to first give more attention the second section, which will be a detailed description of your payment history.

First, look for any errors or inaccuracies that might have been reported. You would be surprised at just how many of those errors can be found in credit reports – insurance companies saying that the deductible wasn't paid, or that payments were late even when they weren't. Find those errors and mark them. These will be the first items you will address when you're trying to boost your score.

Once you have the errors marked, look for anything that might be fraudulent. Items for credit you don't actually have, for example. These could be a sign that your identity has been compromised and should issues you will want to deal with right away.

When you have all the negative aspects of your credit identified, then it is time to develop a plan of action that will help to improve your score. Because we live in a world that is driven by technology and not actually reasoning people, mistakes occur all the time. False information in your report can bring about deep repercussions and will need to be taken care of immediately. It stands to reason that the sooner you find out these mistakes, the sooner you can do what is necessary to restore your good name and boost your credit score.

Your Credit Utilization Ratio

Finally, you want to look at your credit utilization ratio, which is your credit card balance compared to your actual credit limit. It is important to understand that this ratio will make up a significant part of your FICO score, second only to your payment history.

A high ratio indicates that you might actually be overspending and may be getting in over your head in debt. When creditors see this, they will automatically begin to think that you are a high risk of defaulting on your payments.

When you have a good credit utilization ratio, it can be very instrumental in establishing a good credit score and can actually help to balance out some of those negative aspects of your credit; at least until you start working on removing them.

Ideally, the lower your ratio, the better you look on paper. A ratio of 0% means that you are not using any of your available credit. A credit ratio of 30% or less is what creditors are looking for. Anything above that will cause your overall credit score to drop.

CHAPTER 3: Advice to See Success with 609

Whether you want to delete just one thing from your record or you are looking to delete a lot of different things at the same time, you want to make sure that your 609 Letter is taken care of and ready to go. There are a lot of parts that need to go through in order to get this done, but when you look at some of the templates that we have in the next section, you will see that this is not as bad as it may seem.

When you are ready to write out some of the letters you need to send out to the credit agencies, and you are getting all of the documentation ready to go, make sure to follow some of the general advice that we have below:

Basic Guide to Credit Repair

Damaged credit history and low credit scores can throw a big buckle into your financial life.

You're going to have more trouble getting loans and credit cards than those with good credit. If you get a loan or a credit card, you usually pay a higher interest rate than those with higher credit scores. You will still not be eligible for credit cards with the highest rewards and benefits.

But if you have bad credit, don't despair – there are a variety of realistic ways to start reversing your condition and back on track to good credit. There are six main measures involved in the repair of your credit:

- Assess the credit condition
- Dispute incorrect facts about the credit report
- Pay off your loans
- Learn more about healthy credit habits
- Develop a new loan
- **Wait**

You may be able to skip one or two stages, depending on your situation. Even so, it is prudent to recognize the entire mechanism in the event of unforeseen financial challenges recurring in the future.

Step 1: Assess your credit condition

Check your three credit reports and ratings before taking steps to boost your less-than-stellar credit. You need to understand why your credit scores fell in the first place.

You probably already have a clear idea of what happened, whether you skipped credit card payments or you defaulted on a personal loan. Irrespective of that, taking a thorough, truthful look at your financial condition is the first step on the road to high credit. It also offers a valuable opportunity to find and refute incorrect details that could harm your ratings.

Here's an idea of how you're supposed to go about this phase:

1. Check your credit scores. You should be able to check the credit score for each of your reports free of charge. You might be able to display the score with your credit card. If not, many online services can grant you access to a free credit score by simply signing up.

2. Examine your credit reports. Although your credit scores offer a valuable insight into your condition, credit reports provide a comprehensive image that can make it easier to identify the exact issues at play. List any potentially negative details you find, including late payments, collection accounts, requests, and credit cards with high balances relative to their limits.

3. Build an Action Plan. Once you've checked your documentation to decide what you need to do, browse through the steps listed below and resolve each problem with the required solution.

If you think you're too far to work it out on your own, take credit advice. Credit counselors offer credit-related advice that might prove invaluable in helping you navigate the muddy waters of debt.

Step 2: Incorrect Dispute Details

If you discover any inaccuracies when looking through your credit reports, you have the legal right to appeal to them. When you challenge an account, the credit bureau must investigate and delete the item from your credit report if it is not checked as correct.

In certain cases, a deletion could raise your credit score if the deleted item was negative. But even if the deletion doesn't increase your ranking, it's still important to ensure that all information on your records is correct.

For example, a positive mortgage account that doesn't belong to you does not harm your credit score. But it might make it impossible to borrow in the future because it appears like you owe more money than you do on paper.

Disputing a credit report item is fairly easy. Start by deciding which information is incorrect. Then decide which credit office is reporting errors. Follow these moves, eventually:

- **Submit a 609-default letter by certified mail (return receipt requested) to the authorized credit bureau.** Request clarification of the details you believe is inaccurate. Your disagreement would not guarantee the deletion of the information but allows the office to verify the quality of the information.

- **Wait for a reply.** The procedure can take a month or more. After the review, the office should delete the inaccurate details from your credit report if it cannot be checked.

- **If your conflict has not achieved the settlement you were looking for, you have more options.** You can follow up with the office, contact the creditor who supplied the data, make a report to the Consumer Financial Protection Bureau, or even talk to a consumer protection lawyer if the situation so requires.

If you've already found whole accounts that you don't recognize in your credit reports, consider reporting the incident to the FTC and take careful steps to help avoid problems like identity fraud in the future.

We suggest credit screening, even though you haven't found something out of the ordinary in your credit reports. Credit monitoring systems warn you to changes in your credit reports, helping you detect fraudulent accounts and unauthorized access to credit.

If you are disturbed and concerned about theft, you may also want to freeze your credit reports to prevent credit claims from being made on your behalf until your reports have been thawed. All three major credit bureaus must have freezes free of charge.

Credit locks are a different choice. They are similar to freezes but may have more convenient features, such as instant locking/unlocking capabilities.

Step 3: Pay down debts

Paying down your current debts is, at the same time, one of the hardest and most critical aspects of the credit repair process. It's almost always going to take a lot of time, effort, and (of course) money. But once you have made peace with your debts, you may lay the groundwork for future prosperity.

The amount of debt you owe (especially the use of your credit card) is 30 percent of your FICO score. Paying down your credit card debt is also a very successful way to boost your credit score.

Ready to get started, huh? Here are a few solutions for debt reduction:

Pay outright

If your debts are still up or down (meaning you haven't gone to default yet), you might be able to come up with a strategy to start reducing your balances. This can stop bleeding before you get out of control with your credit situation. Sometimes, you can only need to change your budget and prioritize your debt differently.

Set of collection accounts

It's worth mentioning that you should show caution when paying back old collection accounts. If you do not pay the debt, the creditors, and collection companies who buy the debt will have the right to sue you. However, as the debt grows older, it may become time-barred. When the debt has been time-barred, the debt collector will no longer prosecute you.

In every state, the time-barred debt clock is different.

If you make a small payment on a time-barred debt, you will be able to restart the collection clock. In other words, a single payment could open the door to a future lawsuit against your remaining unpaid balance. So, if you're looking to settle an old collection account, it's usually better to wait until you've saved a full, lump-sum settlement balance first. You may need to talk to a consumer debt counsel for advice.

Eventually, even though you pay or settle a collections account, don't expect your credit scores to leap automatically. Unless the lender uses a newer score model (such as FICO 9), paid collections will continue to harm your credit scores as long as the account is on your record.

The good news, though, is that as collections get older, your credit is becoming less and less impacted. Within seven years from the date of default on the original account, all collections must be removed from your credit report.

Step 4: Learn responsible credit habits

When you've got a deal on unpaid loans, late payments, and heavy credit card balances, take the time to inform yourself of the various ways you can make sure you never get to grips with those issues again.

Making all payments in time

This is a little obvious, but you can never miss a loan or a credit card payment unless you can't stop it. Payment history is one of the most influential variables in many models of credit ratings.

Minimum payments are appropriate if you are just trying to prevent late fees, but we highly suggest that you pay your entire credit card balances every month to prevent interest charges (unless you have a 0 percent rate). This applies mainly to transactions, however, as cash advances and balance transfers typically begin to accrue interest immediately.

We also suggest that you trigger automatic payments so that you never have to leave your way to make a payment before its due date. Only keep an eye on your online account to ensure that payments are still made.

Late payments cannot be reported to credit bureaus until they are at least 30 days late, so you can face late fees and/or other repercussions with the lender from the moment you're late.

After the 30-day waiting period has expired, late payment is likely to be reported to consumer credit bureaus. A new late payment on your credit report would almost definitely hurt your credit scores.

Keep your credit card balances down

The ratio of your total credit card debt to your credit limits is called credit utilization. Credit usage plays a crucial role in your credit score. For example, the modern FICO Score 8 calculates 30% of your credit scores from the sums you owed in the credit report category. Your use of credit is the most significant aspect considered here.

Vantage Score 3.0 is taking a different approach. It uses credit usage for 20 percent of its ranking formula and the overall debt for 11 percent. That doesn't mean that the rack up of huge credit card charges during the month would automatically harm you, though. As long as your balances are paid out before the closing date of the statement, your credit utilization ratio should stay low without any harm to your ratings.

Don't borrow more than you can afford

Never borrow so many funds that you can't pay for it in a timely manner. We highly suggest paying off credit card balances in full every month. If you can't stick to paying your credit cards in full every month, you should also stop wiping them out when you're trying to restore your credit.

It's the same with loans. If you're not completely sure you're going to be able to afford a monthly payment without concern, the loan is probably not the right option.

Step 5: Build a new credit

If you've paid off and/or negotiated old debts, you've dealt with incorrect credit details in your reports, and you've built a sound approach to how to deal with credit in the future. You may be able to start creating new credit accounts.

There are a variety of ways to develop new loans. We're going to lead you through some of the best choices, usually available to individuals with low credit scores.

Be an approved consumer

Find a trustworthy friend or family member with a clear history of absolute, on-time payments and ask to be added to his or her credit card account as an approved user.

You can get an approved user card to actually use it, or you can connect it, but you can't give it a card at all. Payment information for your account (positive or negative) will usually also appear on your credit reports either way. Some card issuers do not disclose approved user accounts to the credit bureau.

There may be conditions that prohibit you from being an approved consumer. However, there is usually no need for a credit check.

Open your credit card

There are some credit cards that you are likely to apply for, even though your credit scores are very poor. Most of them have been secured.

Sure, you can need to make a refundable deposit and pay for a card that lacks rewards and benefits. However, credit cards are also among the most valuable tools to restore credit.

Try a loan from a credit builder

Credit builder loans are designed to help you build or repair your loan. You make equal monthly payments all the way through the life of the loan, but you don't get the cash upfront. Instead, you will collect the funds after the balance is paid out in full. Usually, you're going to have to pay interest and some penalties, but none of them appears to be too high.

Credit builders' loans can be very useful on their own. They also fit well alongside other strategies, such as secured credit cards. Using both forms of credit together adds to your wide range of accounts, and a good combination of credit will help your ratings.

Step 6: Wait

Generally speaking, the only thing that can eradicate accurate derogatory details from your credit reports is time. Late fees, collection accounts, and other derogatory items will normally stay on your credit records for 7–10 years. In rare situations, you might be able to eliminate legitimate late fees, but you should not be relying on them. There's always nothing to do with negative credit entries except wait until they're deleted from your records.

Luckily, the negative effect of credit information on your credit score continues to decrease as the information gets older. You're definitely going to see your credit scores go up until the information is deleted from your reports (all other factors being equal), but there's a fair chance they're going to rise progressively even before that.

It will also take time to feel the benefits of your new accounts and good actions. The trick is to be careful and stick to your plans. While remaining responsible, even those with the worst credits will ultimately apply for attractive loans and better credit cards at high rates.

Understanding Credit Repair

We all know that your credit score is one of the greatest determinants of the kind of lifestyle you are likely to lead; that's why we do everything in our power to ensure that we keep it favorable because that in itself determines how much it would cost us to borrow.

It is your right to have correct information reported on your credit report. Why would anybody want to have bad credit owing to wrong and erroneous entries? Is it fair for the individual to have a bad score without any mistakes of his own? Of course not! And for this, you need to take the right steps to fix your bad credit rating. Actually, the Fair Credit Reporting Act (1971) clearly puts it that you have the right to dispute entries in your credit report. You also have a right to get a free copy of your credit report every year, which means that you can check what information has been included in your credit report within that period.

Although the law doesn't clearly tell you to dispute incorrect, erroneous and unverifiable entries, the fact that you have the free copy of your credit report means that you can identify anything that you are uncomfortable with and file a dispute. This is only meant to help you with your credit score and make you more reliable to creditors. You cannot sit back and wait for your credit to fix itself and as soon as you spot errors, you must get to having them fixed.

This coupled with the fact that the FTC clearly states that you can **improve your credit score by yourself** means that all hope is not lost as far as fixing your credit is concerned. Even if the law doesn't tell you to file a dispute if you find any erroneous, inaccurate and unverifiable entries in your credit report, it provides an enabling environment for you to dispute. So you can start to approach the authorities to help you have the errors removed or your score fixed through some means.

For instance, the fact that numerous laws have been put in place to enable credit providers to deal with identify theft and fraud alerts means that you really have some legal backing to ensure that accurate information is published on your credit report. It is your right to have

143

the right score and no one can stop you from having the correct figures mentioned.

The Fair Credit Reporting Act clearly states that it is the duty of every creditor to validate the accuracy or validity of any data contained in a credit report once a credit consumer disputes that information. This means that once you file a dispute on erroneous, inaccurate or unverifiable entries, the creditor will have to validate it or have it removed from the report. This will automatically help you fix your credit score.

Many people wonder if this validation will show badly but it will not. If some erroneous entries were made without your knowledge then you have all the right to challenge it and have it fixed. It will not show badly on your part as you only did something that was necessary for you to rectify a mistake.

I know that sounds fairly straight forward! However, keep in mind that neither the credit reporting agencies nor the credit providers have any interest in having your credit score looking exceptionally good. So they will not jump to help you or themselves take the initiative to fix your problem.

The truth is they make more money when your credit score is bad so why would they want you to have a great credit score when they stand to lose revenues in the process? Everybody thinks for themselves in this world and your creditor will do the same. As long as your account will show bad credit, he or she will be glad to serve you and pull as much money from you as possible. But if they have a chance to help you fix your bad score then they will be least bothered as it will affect their business.

All credit reporting agencies are privately owned multibillion-dollar corporations whose number one priority is profits; they care less about you having a good FICO score. This means that they will definitely want to sabotage your efforts geared towards disputing entries in the credit report; that's why I compiled this book to help you get through the entire dispute process easily and allow you a chance to take the right steps in fixing your bad credit. But do not panic. Although they will put

144

in efforts to block yours, they might not always succeed. You are in the right and they are in the wrong, so it will be easier for you to win the battle. You need to take the right steps and you will get a chance to fix your bad credit score.

To start with, you have to understand how the credit system works, how you can beat the OCR and e-OSCAR computer systems that the credit reporting agencies use, how to use the Fair Credit Reporting Act to your benefit and how to use other effective credit repair strategies to fix your credit. Many times, just fixing your mistakes will do the trick and your credit score will improve instantly. Add to it getting rid of any erroneous entries and you will have a chance to have an extremely high credit score. In any case, you are the only one who has interests in keeping your credit score high so you have to know how to do everything on your own!

So, you now understand why you have to keep your credit score high and some basics on whether it is possible to repair your credit. You must remain determined to have your credit fixed no matter what the circumstances. However, it is one thing to know that the law is on your side as far as disputing inaccurate, unverifiable and erroneous entries is concerned and another to actually get those entries removed from your credit report. Just by noticing that there is a mistake will not help it in getting solved.

You need to take steps to correct it. It will be quite a process and you will have to gear all your efforts towards cleaning your credit score. It can sound like a daunting task but you need to do it in order to avail a good score. To enable you a clear understanding, let me explain how this is so by showing you how the credit system works.

Credit Score Myths Explained

There are a ton of credit score myths out there, and I don't want you to be fooled. Because in the game of raising your credit score, falling prey to the wrong myth could cost you valuable points on your credit score!

1. A Higher Income Will Raise My Credit Score

In actuality, your income has absolutely zero effect on your credit score. Not everyone has the earning power of Donald Trump, and it's only fair that we are not judged based on how much we earn. What's important to lenders is not what you earn, but how you handle your financial obligations.

2. 'X' Number of Credit Accounts Is Too Many

According to FICO, there is no magic number of credit accounts that is too many. Every person's credit history is different, and consequently, the number of credit accounts that is too many is not set in stone. So don't let anyone tell you different!

Tom is able to maintain his high credit score with seven credit cards, two lines of credit, and five mortgages. But he uses only a small percentage of available credit on his credit cards plus pays them off in full each month. He does not use his lines of credit since they are only for emergencies. And the mortgages are for his investment properties and the payments are always submitted on time.

James has a bunch of credit cards, plus more than one line of credit and mortgages too — but his credit score is low. He has five credit cards that are maxed out (plus he often misses payments), and two lines of credit that are also maxed out. His mortgage payment for his home was 60 days late last time. And at least once a year he's late making the mortgage payment for his cabin in the woods.

In this scenario, Tom has more credit accounts but has a higher score.

146

Anna has six credit cards that are all maxed out, and she's been late making payments on and off for the past year. She also has a car loan but just barely manages to scrape up enough money to make the payments each month.

Melanie has one credit card, only uses a small percentage of her available balance, and always pays it off on time. She also has a small car loan for which payments are made on time, every time.

In this case, it is Melanie, with the lower number of credit accounts, who has a higher score.

So if you remember nothing else, remember this: The number of accounts you have is less important than what you do with them.

3. Rent is Reported on My Credit Report

The only time your rent could affect your credit report is if you don't pay it and your landlord gets a judgment against you or sends it to a collection agency. That being said, most lenders do take into account mortgage or rent payments when trying to decide if you qualify for their loan product — it's just that this information does not come from your credit report.

4. Cell Phone Payments Are Reported on My Credit Report

It turns out that most cell phone companies don't bother to report to the credit reporting agencies. The exception to this rule is if you don't make the payments and they're sent to a collection agency — that, on the other hand, is very likely to show up on your credit report.

5. My Full Employment History Is on My Credit Report

While your credit report is likely to show the name of your most recent employers, all of the details surrounding your employment will not be there.

6. Closing Old and Inactive Accounts Will Raise My Score

No way! In fact, closing old and inactive accounts might actually lower your score temporarily.

7. Lowering the Credit Limits on My Credit Cards Will Raise My Score

This is another one that gets a big NO WAY! Just as with closing old and inactive accounts, this might actually lower your score.

8. If I Co-Sign on a Loan, It Won't Show Up on My Credit Report

Even though the loan is technically not yours, because you are the lender's "back-up plan" if the other person named on the loan fails to pay, both the loan and payment history will show up on your credit report as if it **is** your loan. So be careful who you co-sign for since any mistakes they make could lower your credit score.

The only way to stop it from showing up on your credit report is to convince the creditor to remove you as a co-signer — but this is easier said than done, so if you ever co-sign on a loan for someone, assume that you're stuck on there until it's 100% paid off!

9. Paying Off Debt Will Boost My Score by X Amount of Points

Don't get me wrong, paying off debt can definitely improve your credit score. But if you ever read something like "pay off your car loan and your credit score will rise by 50 points," assume this is not accurate. Because credit scores are based on so many factors, it's impossible to predict exactly how much of an impact a single change can make. So don't be fooled by those types of promises!

10. My Score Will Drop If I Check My Own Credit

There are two main kinds of credit inquiries: hard and soft.

Hard inquiries generally do lower your credit score. Hard inquiries include those made by your bank before they approve you for your mortgage, or by a credit card company prior to approving you for one of their cards.

Caution: Keep in mind that checking your own credit score is only a soft inquiry if you order it directly via an approved site such as **www.AnnualCreditReport.com,** or via one of the credit bureaus and their affiliated sites. Whereas if you ask your banker to check the score for you, then it will likely count as a hard inquiry, and will lower it.

11. When I Get Married, the Credit Reports of My Spouse and Myself Will Merge

If you value your independence, you'll be happy to know that getting married does not mean giving up your individual credit score. You keep yours, and your spouse keeps theirs. One does not affect the other. However, keep in mind that if you take on joint debts, such as a mortgage, then that mortgage and its payment history will show up on both of your credit reports.

12. Shopping for a Loan Will Lower My Credit Score

Have you ever tried to do the responsible thing by shopping around for the best rate, and worried that you'd be unfairly penalized for doing so due to all those people checking your credit in a short period of time? Worry no more, my friend!

It turns out that the credit reporting agencies are smart enough to know that this is not a big deal. If all of the inquiries are made in a short amount of time, they will usually appear as only one hard inquiry on your report (sometimes two). VantageScore even goes so far as to say that they count all inquiries made within a 14 day period as a single inquiry. So there you go!

13. If I Always Pay My Bills on Time, I'll Have a Perfect Credit Score

It turns out that just paying your bills on time is not enough to guarantee a perfect score. You also have to maintain a desirable mix of credit accounts, have a history of sufficient length, and have an optimal ratio of debt to available credit, among other things. You're not alone if this bums you out — many people are surprised by this one.
But the good news is that anything over 750 is considered excellent. And whether you have a score of 750, or a perfect 850, you're highly likely to get the same great rates when applying for credit.

CHAPTER 4: How to Proceed with the Letters

Now that we know a little bit more about the Section 609 and how we are able to use this for some of our own needs when it is time to handle our credit report and get the different parts to increase, it is time to look at how we can proceed with these letters.

In the following section, we are going to take a look at the steps that you can utilize in order to write out one of these Section 609 letters. But then it is time to figure out what we want to do with them when the letter is written. There are a few different ways that we are able to make sure these letters get back to the right parties, and we are going to take a look at all of them below:

Emails

Our world seems to run online all the time, and finding ways to work on our credit scores and not have to waste a lot of time copying things or worrying about the paper trails can seem like a great idea. And in some cases, we may find that sending in our 609 letters through email is going to be the best situation for our needs.

Before you do this, though, make sure that you take the time and do the proper research. You want the forms to end up in the right locations, rather than getting sent to the wrong departments, and not doing anything for you in the process. Most of the time there will be listings for the various departments that you want to handle and work with for each credit agency, so take a look at those.

Again, when you are ready, you need to have as many details ready to go for this as possible. Just sending in a few lines about the process and thinking that will get things done is foolish. Write out a letter just like you would if you planned to send these by mail, and use that as the main body of your email. Mention Section 609 and some of the disputes that you want to bring up.

In addition to this, you need to take some time adding in the other details. Attach some ways to prove your identity to the email, along with a copy of the credit report that has been highlighted to show what is going on and what you would like to dispute. Add in any of the other documentation that is needed to help support your case, and have it as clean and organized as possible to make sure the right people can find it and will utilize this information to help you out.

Doing it All Online

Many of the credit agencies have made it easier to go through and work on some of these claims online. This helps you out because you will not need to go through and print it all off or worry about finding the paperwork or printing a bunch of things off. And if you are already on your credit report, your identification has been taken care of.

Since so many people are online these days, doing this right from the credit report is a simple and easy process to work with, and you will catch onto it fairly quickly. Don't take the easy way out with this. If you just click on the part that you think is wrong and submit a claim on it, this is not enough. There won't be any reference back to Section 609, and you will not be able to get them to necessarily follow the rules that come with Section 609.

This is where being detailed is going to be useful in the long run. When you do submit one of these claims online, make sure that you write a note with it to talk about Section 609, specifically the part of 609 that you want to reference in this dispute. You can usually attach other forms to document, who you are and why you think these need to be dropped. Treat this just like you would if you tried to mail the information to the credit agency. The more details that you are able to include in this, the better. This will help to build up your case and can make it harder for those items to stay on your credit report for a long period of time. Make sure to mention the 30-day time limit as well.

Telephone

A telephone is one method that you can use, but it is not usually the right one for this kind of process. For example, how easy is it going to be to show the credit agency what your driver's license looks like? You can repeat the number over if you would like, but this process is still a bit more laborious than some of the others and doesn't always work as well as we would hope it could.

However, this is definitely an option that we can use in order to reach the credit agencies, and for some people who are not sure of what their rights are, or would rather talk directly to the individuals in charge about this issue, the telephone can be the right option. Make sure that you have a copy of your credit report in front of you when you start and having some other identification information and more. This will ensure that you are prepared when someone comes on the line to speak with you.

Just like we will show when working on our letter templates, later on, we need to make sure that we speak about the issue at hand, explain our rights, and go through the information on Section 609. There is the possibility that the other side is going to have some questions for you, and they will at least want to go through and verify your identity to make sure they are ready to go. But the same rules apply here, and if you don't get a response within 30 days of that phone call, then the information should be erased.

Keep good records of what is discussed in that conversation, who you talked to during that time, what time and date it was, and so on. This will make it easier to get someone to respond to you and can help us to get this to work in our favor. Also, remember that you will need to repeat these phone calls to all three credit bureaus in order to get your information cleared on all of them.

Mail

Another option that you are able to work with is mail. This is usually a good method to use because it allows you a way to send in all of the information at once. Since you probably already have a physical copy of your SSN, driver's license, the credit report and more, you can get copies of these made pretty quickly, and then send them on with the Section 609 letter that you are working with. This method also allows us a way to go through and circle or highlight the parts of our credit report that we want to point out to the credit reporting agency.

This method is quick and efficient and will make sure that the information gets to the right party. You can try some of the other options, but sometimes this brings up issues like your information getting lost in the spam folder or getting sent to the wrong part. Mail can take some of that out of the way and will ensure that everything gets to the right location at the right time.

Certified Mail

For the most part, you are going to find that working with certified mail is going to be one of the best options that you can choose. This will ensure that the letter gets to the right place and can tell you for certain when the 30-day countdown is going to begin.

If you send this with regular mail, you have to make some guesses on when the letter will arrive at the end address that you want. And sometimes you will be wrong. If there is a delay in the mailing and it gets there too late, then you may start your 30 days too early. On the other hand, if you assume it is going to take so many days and it takes less, you may wait around too long and miss your chance to take this loophole and use it to your advantage.

Certified mail is able to fix this issue. When the credit agency receives the letter, you will get a receipt about that exact date and even the time. This is going to make it so much easier for you to have exact times, and you can add these to your records. There is no more guessing along the way, and you can be sure that this particular loophole is going to work to your advantage.

Another benefit that comes with certified mail is that you make sure that it gets to its location. If you never get a receipt back or get something back that says the letter was rejected or not left at the right place, then you will know about this ahead of time. On the other hand, if it does get to its location, you will know this and have proof of it for later use. Sometimes things get lost. But you want to be on the winning side of that one. If the credit agency says that they did not receive the letter, you will have proof that you sent it and that someone within the business received it and signed for it. Whether the company lost it along the way, or they are trying to be nefarious and not fix the issue for you, the certified mail will help you to get it all to work for you.

When it comes to worrying about those 30 days and how it will affect you, having it all in writing and receipts to show what you have done and when it is going to be important, this can take out some of the guesswork in the process and will ensure that you are actually going to get things to work for you if the 30 days have come and gone, and no one will be able to come back and say that you didn't follow the right procedures.

As we can see, there are a few different options that we are able to use when it comes to sending out our Section 609 letters.

CHAPTER 5: The 5 Templates You Need

Template 1

We also want to make sure that you can have as many of these templates available that work for you. You could try sending a different one to each of the three credit agencies if that works the best for you, or you can choose to send the same one to all three. No matter what options you are considering here, we need to make sure that we are able to get a lot of choices in the process. Here is the first template letter that you can consider using for your needs.

Date

Your Name

Your Address

Your current city, state, and zip code.

Complain Department

Name of Credit Bureau (You can pick which one goes here)

Address

Dear Sir or Madam

I Take this time to identify all of the items that you would like to dispute, going by the name of the source including whether they come from a tax court or creditors and so on. You can even identify the type of item that you refer to, such as a judgment, a credit account, and more.

Please take the time to investigate this matter and delete the disputed items. As per Section 609 mentioned above, you have 30 days from the receipt of this letter to respond, or the item must be removed. I appreciate your speed in this matter.

Sincerely

[Add your signature to this part]

[Print your name here]

*Make sure that you attach copies of your proof of identity, including your birth date, name, SSN, and your current mailing address. You also want to attach a copy of your credit report, making sure that you highlighted all of the relevant items to make it easier for the interested parties to see what you are talking about.

Template 2

This is the primary format that we will invest some energy in. It will incorporate the entirety of the various parts that you need to get the message to the correct gatherings, and it is quite basic. Recollect that this is only a layout, and we can go through and utilize this as a guide or a blueprint. On the off chance that it doesn't by and large coordinate with what you need, you can roll out certain improvements, or you can decide to utilize one of different layouts that we will have accessible.

Name

Address

Telephone Number

Record # (make a point to incorporate this on the off chance that you have that data).

Name of the Company Contacting/Point of Contact Person

Important Department

Address

Date

Dear [Include the name of the credit revealing office or utilize the name of the contact party in the event that you approach this information]

I'm composing today to practice my entitlement to scrutinize the legitimacy of the obligation your office claims I owe, compliant with the FCRA, Fair Credit Reporting Act.

As expressed in Section 609 of the FCRA, (2) €:

"A customer revealing office isn't needed to eliminate precise harsh data from a purchaser's record except if the data is obsolete under Section 609 or can't be checked."

Just like my right, I am mentioning confirmation of the accompanying things:

[This is the place where we will list any of the things that we are hoping to debate, including the entirety of the record names and numbers that have been recorded with your credit report]

Furthermore, I have featured these things on the joined duplicate of the credit report I got.

I demand that all future correspondence be done through the mail or email. As expressed in the FCRA, you are needed to react to my debate inside 30 days of receipt of this letter. In the event that you neglect to offer a reaction, all contested data should be erased.

Much obliged to you for your brief regard for this matter.

Earnestly,

[Add your mark to this part]

[Print your name here]

See appended; [This is the place where you will rattle off the entirety of the archives that you will connect with this letter]

*Make sure that you join duplicates of your verification of personality, including your introduction to the world date, name, SSN, and your present street number. You additionally need to join a duplicate of your credit report, ensuring that you featured the entirety of the significant things to make it simpler for the invested individuals to perceive what you are discussing.

Template 3

There are a ton of times when the primary format that we talked about will be sufficient for your necessities and can assist you with completing the entirety of the work. Then again, it could be conceivable that you need to discuss the debate in an alternate way, or you just didn't care for the arrangement or something different about the other layout that we went through. That is okay. The accompanying layout will be the one that we can work with too. It discusses a ton of the very issues that we did above however will have a couple of different parts added to it to make this work too. The third format that we can work with incorporates:

Name

Address

Telephone Number

Record # (make a point to incorporate this in the event that you have that data).

Name of the Company Contacting/Point of Contact Person

Important Department

Address

Date

Dear Sir or Madam

I'm writing to practice my entitlement to debate the accompanying things on my document. I have caused a note of these things on the joined duplicate of the report I to have gotten from your organization. You will likewise discover connected duplicates of reports that help to show my personality, SSN, birthdate, and current location.

As expressed in the FCRA, or Fair Credit Reporting Act, Section 609:

[This will be the segment where we incorporate a couple of pertinent statements that depend on what space of Section 609 you might want to debate at that point. You can return to the past section to perceive what a portion of these statements are about, or you can go to the FTC's site to get the authority report that has the specific verbiage that you need. Recollect that you need to note which of the sub-segments you are citing from as well].

The things that I wish to question are as per the following:

1.   [This is the part where you will incorporate however many significant things as you can. You can have up to 20, yet attempt to just work with the ones that bode well for you].

2.   [Keep as a main priority that the subtleties will be the most significant with this one. You need to incorporate the name and the quantity of the record, as recorded on your credit report]

These are [inaccurate, wrong, unverified] because of the absence of approval by various gatherings that is needed by Section 609. I have appended duplicates of important documentation.

I would see the value in your help with researching this way inside the following 30 days. As needed by the FCRA, on the off chance that you neglect to do as such, all previously mentioned data/questioned things should be erased from the report.

Genuinely:

[Add your mark to this part]

[Print your name here]

See connected; [This is the place where you will drill down the entirety of the records that you will append with this letter]

*Make sure that you append duplicates of your verification of personality, including your introduction to the world date, name, SSN, and your present postage information. You likewise need to connect a duplicate of your credit report, ensuring that you featured the entirety of the significant things to make it simpler for the invested individuals to perceive what you are discussing.

Template 4

We have investigated some truly genuine instances of the format that you can use with regards to working with Section 609 and ensuring that you can get the credit offices to delete a portion of the awful stuff that is on your reports and causing you a ton of issues en route. In any case, we will investigate a fouth layout that we can use also.

You will see that this one will be really like what we have done in the last two, yet there are some various approaches to introduce the data and various words that are being utilized also. We should investigate this model and perceive how it very well may be comparable or not the same as the other two layouts that we are working with:

Name

Address

Telephone Number

Record # (make a point to incorporate this in the event that you have that data).

Name of the Company Contacting/Point of Contact Person

Applicable Department

Address

Date

To the responsible party in question,

This letter is a proper debate as per the Fair Credit Reporting Act (FCRA).

Endless supply of my credit report, I have discovered that there are a few off base and unconfirmed things. These have adversely affected my present capacity to get credit, and have given pointless shame and bother.

As I am certain you know, it is my right, as indicated by Section 609 of the FCRA, to demand a legitimate examination concerning these errors. Specifically, I am referring to Section 609 (c) (B) (iii), which records "the privilege of a purchaser to question data in the document of the buyer" under the "model synopsis of the privileges of shoppers."

All things considered, coming up next are things I wish to question on my credit report:

1. [This is the part where you will incorporate however many applicable things as you have. You can do up to 20. Ensure that you incorporate the name and the number that is recorded on each record on this report.]

I have additionally featured the entirety of the things that are pertinent to the appended duplicate of the said credit report.

As expressed in the FCRA, you are needed to react to my debate inside 30 days of receipt of this letter. In the event that you neglect to offer a reaction, all contested data should be erased. I have connected all the significant documentation for your audit. I thank you ahead of time for your brief reaction and goal of this issue.

Truly

[Add your mark to this part]

[Print your name here]

See joined; [This is the place where you will drill down the entirety

*Make sure that you connect duplicates of your evidence of character, including your introduction to the world date, name, SSN, and your present street number. You additionally need to connect a duplicate of your credit report, ensuring that you featured the entirety of the applicable things to make it simpler for the invested individuals to perceive what you are discussing.

Template 5

This will be a somewhat unique sort of letter than what we saw previously. This will be significant in light of the fact that it assists us with following up on the off chance that we have not heard a single thing from the other party. Recall that we are allowing them 30 days to go through and give us a reaction or the like, or they naturally need to take that off their reports. The 30 days starts when they get the letter you send, not when you compose it or when you send it. This is another motivation behind why it is critical to go through and get it sent through confirmed mail, so you have a precise date close by.

At the point when the 30 days are finished with, the time has come to do a subsequent letter. This will be the point at which you let the organization realize that the 30 days are finished and that you anticipate that things on your report should be deleted and finished with as quickly as time permits. That is the reason we will work with the accompanying to assist us with composing the subsequent letter that we need.

Name

Address

Telephone Number

Record # (make a point to incorporate this in the event that you have that data).

Name of the Company Contacting/Point of Contact Person

Important Department

Address

Date

Dear Sir or Madam

My name is [Your name], and I contacted you a little while back in regards surprisingly report. This letter is to inform you that you have not reacted to my underlying letter, dated [insert date]. I have repeated the provisions of my question beneath for your benefit.

[This is the place where we will embed data from the letter we expounded initially on the contested things. Incorporate questioned account names and numbers as recorded on your credit report.]

Area 609 of the FCRA states that you should explore my debate inside 30 schedule days from my underlying letter. As you have neglected to do as such, I generously demand that you eliminate the previously mentioned things from my credit report.

Any further remarks or questions can be coordinated to my lawful delegate, [insert name], and I can be reached at [insert telephone number].

Genuinely

[Add your mark to this part]

[Print your name here]

See joined; [This is the place where you will rattle off the entirety of the reports that you will connect with this letter]

*Make sure that you connect duplicates of your evidence of character, including your introduction to the world date, name, SSN, and your present street number. You additionally need to append a duplicate of your credit report, ensuring that you featured the entirety of the pertinent things to make it simpler for the invested individuals to perceive what you are discussing

CHAPTER 6: Conclusion

After this guide, you should have enough confidence to take complete control of your financial status and your credit report. It must have been very difficult for you to delete things from your credit report, or you have given up on the fact that it is impossible to raise your credit score. I've made sure you're going to be so confident with the guide that you can take things out of your credit report. Your credit score goes hand-in-hand with your financial security, and there's nothing more rewarding than living a stable life. You should be able to know and assess what your credit score is and how you can improve it. You should be able to know what to do while fixing your credit score, and even what not to do with it.

You can try out the creditors, and you can do so by sending letters of goodwill, with the promises I made to help you increase your FICO score, and also to fix your credit. You should be able to do that, because I've made a guide to that in the book, and I've also helped you increase your credit score to over 800, which is exceptional. Today's credit background is what will decide whether you're going to get a loan, a career, or even a recommendation. If you've got a poor credit history, it's really going to be terrible if you don't follow the guide I gave it to you. The main purpose of the book is to help you conquer the fear and negativity; if you want to obtain the highest credit score, you need to believe in yourself that you can manage it and raise it to more than 800. The models are in order to help you make those improvements, a guide for how to write a conflict letter and a 609-credit repair letter. The guide is there to help you stabilize your credit history and your financial future.

CPSIA information can be obtained
at www.ICGtesting.com
Printed in the USA
LVHW010515140521
687424LV00009B/976